Soul  Awakenings

Exploring the Spiritual Journeys of One Hundred Women

April 26, 2008

Dear Laurie,
It was a pleasure to be your instructor for Nursing 6208 in the graduate program at Dominican University! Wish you the best!

Michelle Quigley Martinez

MICHELLE A. QUIGLEY

04 05 06 07 HH 10 9 8 7 6 5 4 3 2 1
Printed in the United States of America
ISBN: 0-9744149-2-1
Library of Congress Control #: 2003113526

Requests for permission to make copies of any part of this work can be made to:

Cameo Publications, LLC
PO Box 8006
Hilton Head Island, SC 29938
1-866-372-2636
publisher@cameopublications.com
www.cameopublications.com

SEL032000 SELF-HELP / Spiritual
OCC036000 BODY, MIND & SPIRIT / Spirituality / General
SOC028000
SOCIAL SCIENCE / Women's Studies
OCC019000
BODY, MIND & SPIRIT / Inspiration & Personal Growth

Cover and text pages designed by David Josephson
Author photo by veraphotography.com
Hair by Jane from Salon Des Artistes in Sausalito, California

This book is dedicated to my parents,
Anne and Nicholas Quigley,
Who are now with the angels.
They taught my sister Victoria
and me the meaning of spirituality
by living and experiencing it.
"Thank you, Mom and Dad,
from my heart and my soul."

About the Author

Michelle A. Quigley is a registered nurse. She received her Bachelor of Science degree in nursing from Governors State University in University Park, Illinois and received her Master of Science degree in nursing administration from the University of Illinois in Chicago.

Michelle has worked closely with women throughout her career in health care. She gained much insight into the personalities of women and developed a new interest centering on spirituality. After spending over thirty years in management, writing several articles and conducting several presentations, Michelle embarked on her own spiritual journey, which was the catalyst for this book.

Throughout her own spiritual journey, not only did she learn from God and herself, but she also reached out to others in the process.

Michelle currently resides in California with her husband Jose.

Acknowledgements

First and foremost, I wish to express my boundless gratitude to the one hundred women who gave a part of their souls.

A very special thanks to Nancy Grenat for your encouragement, support and, most of all, belief in my dream to write this book on women and spirituality. You were there from the beginning and throughout with your willingness to listen. You truly are a gift from God, my dear friend.

Particular thanks and praise to several special people:

Pamela Gonyaw for being my spiritual catalyst and introducing me to the "Ladies from Georgia."

Diana Luskin Biordi, Ph.D., R.N., for your encouragement and research expertise.

Patricia D. Padjen for your beautiful enthusiasm and eagerness to read the finished manuscript.

Victoria Quigley Forbes, my sister, for believing in my dream and introducing me to the women from Quincy.

Robert F. Molchanov for introducing me to thirty wonderful women.

Father Thomas Healy and Sister Rita Specht, R.S.M. from Our Lady Of Mount Carmel Church, Chicago, Illinois for allowing me the opportunity to speak at a Rite Of Christian Initiation Of Adults meeting in hope of recruiting grandmothers, mothers, aunts and sisters for interviews.

Janet Horner Lanier for welcoming me into your Denver home and introducing me to the "Women from Colorado."

Christine Shimkus for our special bond of friendship. You never doubted that my dream for this book would become a reality.

Sally Stefula Frankowski for our cherished friendship since we were five years old. Thank you for your support, joy for life and your love for all living creatures. It's a pure pleasure to know you.

The Discalced Carmelite nuns for your prayers and intercession.

Dawn Josephson, my editor, for believing in this book. Thank you for understanding.

All the wonderful people I met along the way. I have been blessed by your encouragement, support, and interest for a book on women and spirituality.

Last, and most important, I wish to express my unending love and gratitude to my husband, Jose Miguel Martinez. The love of my life. Thank you, Jose, for recognizing my soul and taking my hand as we continue on our spiritual journey together.

Dear God, you are truly awesome! Thank You!

Table of Contents

Introduction

Welcome to *Soul Awakenings*. This book is based on conversations I have had with one hundred women on the topic of spirituality. It is a description of their spiritual journeys and how they balance their spirituality with their everyday lives.

I chose not to include those presently in a religious role, such as a nun or a minister, as they have "consciously" selected their spiritual lives. Instead, I sought a perspective from the ordinary woman, one who rises in the morning; puts on her sneakers, heels, sandals, or boots; and manages to get through the day. You will discover as I did that "the ordinary is not ordinary at all; rather, it is quite extraordinary."

I chose to write a book about women and spirituality for many reasons. For a long time, I had an inner driving force to write a book about women, but I was not clear on the precise subject matter. I remember one afternoon in 1988 walking along the lakefront in Chicago with my dear friend Nancy, explaining to her my inner drive. She gave me magnificent encouragement to write my book and follow my instinct. At the same time, I had found myself at the crossroads of my life and praying for an answer. God answered my prayers in an unforeseen way to me, and those crossroads became a catalyst and caused deep spiritual searching on my part.

During my search I found other women, likeness of souls, who were also on their spiritual journeys. I discovered that spirituality was extremely important to them. So in 1990 I decided to interview one hundred women on the topic of spirituality. The interview process began in January 1991 and ended that same year. Initially, I interviewed my friends, colleagues, and people I knew from various women's groups. But then the word spread. Before long, my phone rang day and night with calls from women requesting me to interview them for the book.

I remember walking through Fort Mountain State Park, in the northwest mountains of Georgia, with my friend Pam who was inquiring about how the interviews were progressing. While we were talking, several women nearby overheard our conversation and joined in. At the end of our afternoon climb and drive home, all of us exchanged telephone numbers and proceeded to our individual homes. By the time Pam and I had reached her home, three messages were on her answering machine from the women we had just met. They were requesting that I interview them for the book too!

Then there was my dear friend Jan from Denver, Colorado who called me at my home in Chicago to inform me that she had mentioned the idea of my book to some of the women she worked with. Fifteen women requested to be interviewed. So I flew out to Denver. The book took on its own energy...the energy of the women's souls...the force of God.

I quickly discovered how open and willing the women were to talk to me about spirituality. Some of the women never had the opportunity to describe the depth of their own being to another person. Many of them told me, "I never talked about spirituality with anyone before."

I remember interviewing a ninety-one-year-old woman who told me sadly that all the members of her family had passed away. Thank God that her friends remained.

Another time, I was sitting on the living room floor rocking a baby in my arms, with the family dog beside me, as the infant's mother, with tears rolling down her face, told me about her difficult bed-bound pregnancy and that the baby I was holding was a miracle.

A twenty-eight-year-old young lady interviewee requested that I please talk to her eighty-seven-year-old grandmother.

And a fifty-one-year-old mother requested that I interview her twenty-three-year-old daughter. These women inherently knew the importance of getting the message from various perspectives.

What amazed me most was that here I was a complete stranger to the majority of the women, yet they freely opened their souls to me. It's now apparent to me that all of us, like these one hundred women, need the same opportunity once in our lives to describe what we truly are to someone. It is such an awareness of one's soul and such a catharsis. During the interviews, the women talked about their childhood, growing up, their trials, and their joys. Laughter, tears, and hugs all emerged from the hundreds of hours of interviewing. I will always cherish the moments I had with each of the women.

I present the women and their messages to you in a contemporary, personal, heart-felt fashion, which will richly enhance your life. The women range in age from twenty-three to ninety-one. They come from various walks of life, cultures, and locales, encompassing eleven states plus Washington, D.C. They are real and very much like you and me.

The taped interviews consisted of discussions around twenty-five questions, which were not available to the women prior to their interviews. There were no "right" or "wrong" answers. The responses came from within the women and were based on their levels of maturity and various life experiences.

I hand transcribed each interview personally, because I needed to feel, hear, and encompass in my being their special soul messages for you. After each interview, I discovered that I was fantastically energized and never, never emotionally drained. It was a fabulous state of being.

Some of the women during or after their interviews told me that they had felt the same energy. "I felt my spirituality here," they said. "I felt a white light around us," some proclaimed. As one woman put it, it was a time of "women doing something for women!"

While I was in the interviewing phase of this book, I was experiencing a trying time in my own life. My father had just passed away and I was working long hours at the University of

Chicago Hospitals and struggling with the medical management of my diabetes. Many times I found myself reading the handwritten transcripts of the interviews to receive inspiration and comfort from the women's words. My dream is that when you read this book it will do the same for you.

Although I have chosen to speak directly to women about spirituality, the subject is no less relevant to men, and I also invite them to read this book.

This is a special invitation to everyone. Join us in our soul journeys. Keep your mind open. Read with your heart. Let your soul be touched.

Chapter One
Our Spiritual Thread

"Spirituality is part of my life, and it's not just playing a part. Rather than a thread that is woven through the fabric on its own, it is the thread that holds the fabric together. Without the thread, the material falls apart."

Julianne

A special thread binds all women together, and I call this our *spiritual thread*. We are not isolated from the whole of mankind, nor do we work in solitude. Instead, we experience the world in the female form and with a woman's spirit; therefore, we have a different perspective. Our souls reach out to like souls, other women in the universe, and we become a sisterhood of women that binds us together. We understand each other. We cry with each other. We support each other. We are not alone.

As a woman and professional nurse for over thirty years, I have had the opportunity to witness numerous situations in which women have demonstrated remarkable courage and strength. The more I interacted with women on a daily basis, the more I realized that when women were involved in situations such as birth, illness, trauma, and death, they drew from an inner strength and peace to sustain them through their challenge. Their actions made a distinct impression on me, because in the midst of the chaos and frenzy of the hospital, these women displayed a sense of calmness that stood out. Here they were, ordinary women in extraordinary circumstances, yet they triumphed over their situation in an almost stoical way and often acted as the comforter to their grieving family members. Their behavior intrigued me and prompted me to begin my quest into this topic of spirituality.

In this book you will find women who exemplify "every woman." Their insights will recharge your faith in mankind, because their words will give you both strength and comfort. They prove that there is a strength we can only receive from other women.

For a moment, reflect on the numerous conversations you have had with other women about the struggles they have experienced. Can you remember how often you have heard or made statements such as:

"How does she do it? You have to admire her. A single parent raising three young children on her own."

"She had a hectic work schedule all day. And did you see how loving she was with her elderly father later that evening?"

"She is a remarkable woman! She has never had it easy in her life. Yet, she never complains."

They all sound so familiar.

Women today live in complex, ever changing environments that place constant demands on our energies and souls. Between family, work, community, and self, we are pulled simultaneously in various directions. Therefore, we women often find ourselves wearing many different hats . . . mother, wife, sister, friend, and many more. Through all of this, we still strive to be loving, caring, and comforting to our children, families, friends, and co-workers.

How do we as women survive and maintain this balance? Where do we receive our strength to face the multi-dimensional arenas in our lives? How is it that so many women manage to wear these various hats in their lives and still smile and exude an inner strength and warmth throughout the day?

The answer for me and many women is the essence of this book. From the interviews, it is apparent to me that "our spiritual thread" is woven throughout our conversations and it is clearly our bedrock. We women pull from within and from our own inner spirituality every day.

But what is this "inner spirituality?" How does it relate to God? Can we describe it?

How did we learn about spirituality? Did a significant female person in our lives teach us? A mother? A grandmother? An aunt? A sister? A girlfriend? Was there a significant male person in our lives who taught us? A father? A grandfather? A husband? A brother? A friend? How do we express it? Does it make a difference in our lives? With relationships?

Would other women want to share their thoughts about their inner spirituality? About their relationship with God? What advice would they like to pass on to other women? To men? And what does all this mean to you, the reader?

The answers to all these questions and more are in the following pages. As you read the chapters, you will find numerous common spiritual threads that run through each of our lives. You will discover or rediscover what spirituality truly means to a woman.

Chapter Two
The Importance of Spirituality

"When all else fails, spirituality is the one piece that remains consistent." **Hope**

"My spirituality is my lifeline."
"I don't think there is anything more important than spirituality."
"If I don't have my spirituality, how would I cope?"
"Without my spirituality, I die."

These are the responses I received when I asked the one hundred women if spirituality was important to them.

Remarkably, one hundred out of the one hundred women clearly stated that spirituality was important to them. Wow! Few questions receive such a unanimous response. Furthermore, all one hundred women stated that spirituality played a significant part in their lives *and made a difference*. Let me first share with you a few of their responses.

Nancy, a forty-eight-year-old Chicago real estate agent, explained the importance of spirituality. "It's essential," she said. "What else is there? Really! Look at all these pictures of houses on the walls here. They're all for sale. There are a lot of unhappy people. Some of them are for sale because of a divorce or a death in the family. There has to be some strand of continuity that helps me make sense out of my life."

Twenty-seven-year-old Sally emotionally told me, "I don't think I could make it through another day without my spirituality. Having my girlfriend murdered and finding one of my room-mates on the bathroom floor with her wrists cut…I don't know if I would have gotten through that if I didn't have spirituality to turn to. I couldn't have gotten through."

Kathy, a forty-one-year-old woman from Atlanta, Georgia, had a dream one night that brought the importance of spiritual-ity into the forefront for her. She emphasized that the dream is as vivid to her today as the night it occurred. "I had a dream one night about a year ago. I walked into a room and there was a table, two chairs, and Jesus sitting. He said, 'What would it take to make you happy?' I thought about it for a minute. 'Prob-ably the love of a good man and a successful business,' I re-plied. He reached over and put His hand on mine and said, 'But the man can leave and the business can fail. Don't put your trust in the things of the world.'" After a brief pause, Kathy continued, "It doesn't matter what you achieve. In the twinkle of the eye it can disappear. What do you have? What is left? What is really important?"

Evelyn eloquently and simply stated, "Spirituality is real important! I don't think anything in the whole world is more serious than someone putting His life down so that others can live."

As I asked the women this seemingly simple question, "Is spirituality important to you?" my own definition of the concept began to form. I realized that my spirituality *is* the true essence of me. Without it, I don't exist. It's my journey and my con-nectedness with God. Growing up and as a grown woman, I didn't always embrace my spirituality, and as a result I lived with a void inside that I couldn't explain. But once I began thinking about my spirituality and assessing its role in my life, that empty feeling went away and a sense of peace took over.

All women need an opportunity to assess their spirituality. Without a sense of what your spirituality is, you go through life on automatic pilot – you're doing the motions of living, but you're never really experiencing life. Your spirituality is what attracts people into your life. It's the inner peace, the joy, the gusto you feel in everyday activities. Your spirituality gives you the strength to persevere and overcome life's challenges.

Self-Reflection

Think about your answers to the following questions and then take a few moments to do the exercise. Your answers and actions will help you connect with your own spirituality.

Questions for Meditation:

- ✓ Is spirituality important to me? Why or why not?
- ✓ What role does spirituality play in my life?
- ✓ What role would I like spirituality to play in my life?

Exercise: Assess Your Own Spirituality

Find a quiet place in your home or out in nature. Sit in a comfortable position. If it helps you relax, play some soothing background music or light some candles. Do whatever you need to do to get into a relaxed state. Once you feel relaxed and the outside stresses are gone, think back over your life and identify those times when you felt challenged. Perhaps it was during a time of illness, a job loss, or a family death. How did you handle the situation? What did you do to get through it? Assess the specific actions you took or the thoughts you had at the time – that was your spirituality in action. How can you apply the strength you displayed back then to your everyday experiences?

So what is this inner spirituality? How do other women describe it? How does it relate to God? Let's read further to discover what spirituality truly means to a woman.

Chapter Three
A Woman's Meaning of Spirituality

"What is so neat about spirituality is that it feels like a blanket around me." Jean

"Spirituality is the core of who I am."
"It's an awareness of my soul."
"It encompasses God and everything that I feel is love."

This is what spirituality meant to three of the women. Let's explore further.

For me, spirituality always meant my relationship with God – my soul's connection with the Divine. It is a grounding force that helps me make sense out of the various highs and lows in my life. When it is grand, I thank Him. When my journey becomes difficult, I frequently turn to God for strength and support. And when the events seem too intense for me to handle, my conversations with Him become solicitations for His assistance and sometimes very heart-wrenching pleas.

However, as I look upon my spiritual journey to God, I must acknowledge that there has always been one definite factual occurrence – God has always answered my prayers. ALWAYS! He may not have always answered my prayers the way I wanted them to be answered, but he did answer them His way. The most remarkable fact is that God's answers to my problems have always been the best ones for me. Far better than I could ever imagine.

I remember a time in my life when I was out of work and looking for a particular job. I went on many interviews and finally found the position I wanted with a healthcare organization. I prayed to God every night after the successful interview that they would offer me the position. That did not happen. They hired someone else, and I was disappointed. I knew the job was perfect for me and I for it, and I couldn't understand why God didn't listen to me. So I continued interviewing. A few weeks later, out of the blue, I received a call from a nursing colleague whom I hadn't heard from in months. She informed me that a very prestigious healthcare organization had an opening in the upper levels of management. I made a note to myself to send them a resume. Before I did, though, that very same healthcare organization contacted me to inform me about the opening, so I immediately sent in my resume. After the initial interview, I understood why the previous job opportunity was offered to someone else. A week later they called and offered me the position, which I joyfully accepted. I was meant to have this new job with this wonderful organization. It was by all accounts a "dream job." God did listen, and He directed me to what was best for my soul.

Based on my own relationship with God, it was a comforting reassurance for me to hear during my interviews with the women that fifty of them clearly defined spirituality as their "relationship with God." "It is my belief in God," some said. "It is the true essence of who I am because God is part of me," others remarked.

Twenty-five women defined spirituality in a different context, as more of a "personal inner strength." They further explained that many times throughout their day, especially during trying periods, they would consciously pull from within themselves in order to access their inner spirituality. At other times, they explained, it was just "there for them." As one woman said, "It just comes out. I access it, but not consciously." Spirituality was like a well for them in which they drew from throughout their days, consciously or unconsciously, in order to reach their inner selves, their souls.

About one-eighth of the women identified spirituality with their religion, their beliefs, and their religious traditions, which many women can certainly relate to. Remember the Baptisms? First Communions? Bar Mitzvahs? Weddings? Funerals?

As forty-four-year-old Molly from Denver, Colorado told me, "I grew up with organized religion in my family. It was part of our lives, acknowledging the presence of God and that He is always there for you. I don't know if you saw the movie *Guardian Angel*, but in the movie two kids are walking across the bridge and an angel is hovering over them. It is that type of feeling or concept that was there for me as a child. It is still with me."

Peggy, an American Indian woman in her sixties, concurred by saying, "Spirituality is my Indian beliefs. One of the biggest traditions I was taught since my childhood was that the greatest virtue is giving. It is better to give than to receive."

Another distinct meaning the women pointed out was to simply state the obvious. Spirituality is intangible and esoteric, because it comes from the spiritual dimension. "It is what people think is beyond the earth. What's way out there in the world," one woman said. "It comes from an outside force that stays within us," another woman replied.

A few women explained that spirituality meant how they lived their lives. As one woman said, "Spirituality is more a way of life than a ritual or a church." Yet another woman said, "It is how I approach things on a day to day basis."

Another woman concurred: "Spirituality is my life. First thing I do with my mornings is thank God that I am alive, and then I look at my daughter. Spirituality is just like breathing. My heart goes out to people who don't have it."

One of the most comforting meanings of spirituality I heard was from Jean, a thirty-year-old Chicagoan who stated, "Spirituality is my home. It is with me all the time."

Spirituality has a very personal and special meaning to each of the women. Since it is intangible, some of the women found it difficult to define its meaning to me. As one woman explained, "How can I put into words what I feel?" However, all of the women I interviewed were able to describe, whether in specific words or with metaphors, what spirituality personally meant to them. Why? Because we women feel it, struggle with it, live it, and therefore possess the capability to describe it.

It is so important to us and yet so misunderstood. But it shouldn't be, because it is the Divine in us. It is about depth, caring, and love. It is that special spark deep inside, the innate part of each of our souls.

Spirituality is the common thread that binds us together with other women, to mankind, and to the universal light – God. It is at the heart of what it truly means to be a woman.

Self-Reflection

Think about your answers to the following questions and then take a few moments to do the exercise. Your answers and actions will help you better define your own concept of spirituality.

Questions for Meditation:
- ✓ What does spirituality mean to me?
- ✓ What words or phrases can I use to define my spirituality?

Exercise: Put Your Feelings Into Words

Defining a feeling can be a difficult task. The key is to honestly answer direct and focused questions in order to make your feelings more tangible.

Think back to the life events you recalled in the previous exercise. As you relive the moments in your mind, use the following questions to help verbalize what you were feeling at the time. Be specific with your answers. If you can't think of precise words, use metaphors or draw a picture. Do whatever you must to move your feelings into the tangible realm.

- ✓ How is this event a reflection of my spirituality?
- ✓ How did the event impact me?
- ✓ How did I change as a result of the event?
- ✓ What barriers did I overcome?
- ✓ How did I grow from the challenge?

✓ What was the impact on my life?
✓ How did the outcome help other people?
✓ Was it a positive outcome? How?
✓ Was it a negative outcome? How?
✓ Was it just an outcome of surviving? How?

Answering these direct questions in relation to the challenging life event will force you to think of the situation in more spiritual terms. You'll realize that the event may indeed be a reflection of your spirituality as opposed to some other concept.

The fact is that we are spiritual human beings. The more we examine our spirituality, the more we evolve as women. One way to attain that spiritual growth is to ask ourselves direct questions without being afraid of hearing our own answers. The topic of spirituality is not taboo. We women need to honestly answer the direct questions to keep our meaning of spirituality alive.

Chapter Four

Do Women Consider Themselves Spiritual?

"Spirituality is a total awareness of one's life and trying to act from the point of love." **Nancy**

Remarkably, eighty-four of the women I interviewed definitely considered themselves to be spiritual persons. One woman summed up her perception so eloquently by stating, "I don't go out on a limb and preach or do things like that, but I live what I feel."

Carol, a forty-eight-year-old American Indian woman from rural Colorado, said, "I consider my whole life as a spiritual journey. Everything I do in relation to myself and to the outer world is an extension of my spiritual beliefs."

Fourteen women did not reply with a definite yes or no, but they stated they were somewhere in the middle. As a twenty-nine-year-old Chicago registered nurse stated, "I'm not gung-ho religious, spiritual, nor am I in the other direction. I'm kind of in the middle."

Jennifer, a saleswoman, wife, and mother, further explained to me that, "I'm spiritual at certain times. I think of myself as a realist. But there are times when I really think there is something more going on than just nature."

A few women believed that spirituality and inner strength were one and the same; therefore, they spoke within that context. As Angela, who described her occupation as a student and observer of life, explained, "I consider myself to be a strong person. In that sense, I have great faith in a power greater than myself. Without that faith I am nothing. I see it as a source of strength, and that is my spirituality."

A thirty-two-year-old mother, wife, owner of a day care center, and consultant vocalized how her inner strength is challenged daily. "It's questionable at times. There are times I just want to fall apart and let somebody else be strong today. Why can't somebody else do the sixteen things I've done this morning? As I'm aging, I'm getting better at placing my priorities in line. I realize I can't do everything perfectly."

When a few of the women compared themselves to images of what they believed a spiritual woman should be, they did not consider themselves to be spiritual persons. They thought a spiritual woman had to be someone extraordinary, someone who did something unusual or remarkable, someone who was saint-like. They did not consciously realize that each person is extraordinary, unique, and remarkable, thereby making every individual a spiritual being.

Marion, a seventy-four-year-old widow, explained, "Well, I don't really [think I am a spiritual woman], because I suppose I've been so busy. I haven't given up time for prayer as everyone says you should. When I think of a spiritual person, I think of someone who devotes everything in that direction."

A forty-seven-year-old librarian also did not perceive herself to be spiritual, according to her image of a spiritual woman. She further told me, "That was one reason I was wondering whether I should be interviewed tonight, because I don't necessarily consider myself that way. It's nothing that I particularly cultivated. I resisted the idea of being spiritual because I know women who are more that way than I am. They should be classified that way, but I don't really see myself particularly that way."

Only two out of the one hundred women responded with a definite no. As one woman emphatically said, "No. I don't let myself acknowledge that. It's in there, but do I access it consciously? No."

The second women sadly echoed, "Lately, no. I think I used to feel that there were unanswered questions and things I didn't know. Now I care less about those things. In a way it's sad. It's a little hopeless."

But we are all spiritual human beings – each and every one of us, even if we don't consciously acknowledge it, work at developing it, or believe that we are. As Elaine, a forty-three-year-old psychologist from Anchorage, Alaska, simply and eloquently echoed, "I consider everyone to be a spiritual person."

We are all children of God and made in His likeness. Each of us is composed of four dimensions: physical, mental, emotional, and last but most precious and important, spiritual. We seldom have difficulty acknowledging our physical dimension: our body; nor the mental: our minds; nor even our emotional side; but when it comes to our spiritual, it's always a different story. But think of those times when you feel a deep inner peace, an abounding joy, or an unconditional love. That's your spirituality, your soul, and your relationship with God!

Once we women acknowledge and believe that our spirituality is part of our wholeness, our lives take on so much more depth, meaning, and fulfillment. That's because we need all four dimensions – physical, mental, emotional, and spiritual – to be balanced. But spirituality is the first and most important part, because it's the thread that weaves through the other three.

Some women claimed that they were so busy trying to get their physical or emotional needs met that they had no time for spirituality. However, the only way they got through the crisis, the trauma, or the abuse was with that spiritual thread that they pulled through their life, many times without even knowing it. Even though the event may have been challenging and they were so focused on survival, when it was over they each breathed a sigh of relief and said, "Thank you, God." Thus, their spirituality was always there in full force in the background.

As the French philosopher Pierre Teilhard de Chardin inspirationally stated:

"We are not human beings having a spiritual experience. We are spiritual beings having a human experience."

What kind of experience are you having?

Self-Reflection

Think about your answers to the following questions and then take a few moments to do the exercise. Your answers and actions will help you realize your true image of spirituality.

Questions for Meditation:

✓ Do I consider myself to be a spiritual person? Why or why not?

✓ What do I consider a spiritual woman to be?

✓ How do I compare to my image of spirituality?

✓ What can I do to meet that image?

✓ Is that image accurate or even feasible?

Exercise: Fill In the Missing Piece

If you feel that you do not meet your own expectations for what a spiritual woman should be, search deeper for your true image of spirituality. Listen to the little inner voice that tells you what spirituality is. Remember, this is your image of spirituality – not your mother's, not your neighbor's, and not even your church's, even though these outside sources may have helped shaped your spirituality. Be persistent and consistent in your search. Go to bookstores. Read books about spirituality to help shape your image. Go to seminars about spirituality. Go to a café with a trusted friend and talk about spirituality. Have the courage to acknowledge it or talk about it. Have the strength to search for it. Have the belief to keep searching for that inner peace you need. The good news is that once you have it, you have it for the rest of your life. That's how important this step is. Don't give up.

Chapter Five

What Forms a Woman's Spirituality?

"Each one of us in the entire universe has a soul or a spirit connected to the God force. We are in touch with that spirit at different levels. It is the greatest challenge as human beings."

Liz

What forms a woman's spirituality? Are there essential elements to a woman's spiritual formation?

As the women individually answered these questions, I noticed several common elements repeat throughout their responses. Collectively, the women were able to identify eight distinct elements.

As you read their responses, reflect on what forms your spirituality. Maybe one of the women's responses will trigger some thoughts for you in this area. They certainly did for me. Identify the element or elements that form your spirituality. Become aware of them. Cultivate them, even if they are difficult for you, because those special elements will aid you on your journey. Through them you will experience soul growth. Treasure them. Realize how important they are for your soul's formation and your connection to God.

During this process, however, realize that your particular elements may be very different from what the women responded. That's okay, because we're all unique. What may work for one person may not work for another. Therefore, don't take the elements these women indicate as the ultimate truth; rather, use them to guide your thinking so you can determine the essential elements of your own spirituality.

Now, let's hear the women describe these eight elements.

Element One: Relationship With God

Twenty-six of the women clearly told me that their personal relationship with God and the development and strengthening of that relationship were the elements in their lives that made them spiritual.

Toney, a forty-six-year-old mother and wife from Atlanta, Georgia, responded, "I asked Jesus into my life sixteen years ago and He has proceeded to change me ever since. I got closer and closer to Him. It's beautiful."

A forty-eight-year-old woman from Chicago explained how God was there for her. "I believe in God. I had a breast biopsy and they suspected cancer. When I first found out I was very upset. I just couldn't believe there were cancer cells. The surgeons were able to remove them all. I wasn't afraid. I just knew I was going to be okay because of God."

From Quincy, Illinois a forty-three-year-old mother and teacher joyfully said, "I have this wonderful hotline to my Maker. We are so connected! It sure keeps me on the right track."

Nancy, a thirty-eight-year-old registered nurse from Indiana, eloquently told me, "It is that deep innate part of me that is my soul. It is that God spark – the universal spark that is in me. It is tapping into that and being aware of it. Letting that shine through and hopefully functioning from that aspect."

Self-Reflection

Think about your answers to the following questions and then take a few moments to do the exercise. Your answers and actions will help you assess your relationship with God.

Questions for Meditation:

- ✓ What is my relationship with God?
- ✓ Is this relationship important in my life? Why or why not?

✓ What is God to me?

✓ How do I use my relationship with God in my daily life?

Exercise: Trust in God

Having a relationship with God will give you the strength and confidence to move forward with a decision or to overcome a challenge. The more you release your fears and begin to trust in God, the greater "God-energy" you put out that brings what you need into your life. Think back to a time when your release brought into your life what you needed most. Perhaps you were short on cash for the month, only to have a refund check in your mailbox the next day. Maybe you were bogged down at work because your assistant quit, and the perfect job candidate walked in to inquire if you were currently hiring. These are gentle nudges from the Universe that let you know God is with you. Think back over your life and recount all the times similar scenarios happened to you. Remember that feeling of release and the help you unexpectedly received. That's your relationship with God – your trust in God's wisdom.

Element Two: Personal Spiritual Journey

About one-seventh of the women believed that their own spiritual journey, in which they searched for that deep innate part of themselves, their soul, was the special element that formed their spiritual dimension.

From Denver, Molly explained how her spiritual journey became a driving force in her life. "I believe I'm on a journey. I used to think it was outside of me, but I realized it wasn't. The fact is that I want spirituality. It's a desire and a thirst. It's something at times I tried to let go, so that I can devote more of myself to my job or whatever, but it pursues me. I can't!"

Jo had also spoken about her journey. "I don't want to say I'm Sally spiritual, because I'm not. But I'm very serious about the pursuit, relative to understanding myself as I relate to the spiritual dimension. I grabble in the spiritual path and need to discover who I am in this search for a deeper meaning. Even though I was a practicing Methodist, it was just a ritual that seemed very empty. I kept searching for something with a deeper meaning. My pursuit has been taking me into a spiritual journey, which I now realize is a journey for the rest of my life. Although intellectually I believe in a Higher Being, spiritually I am becoming more aware. Every moment is a gift and every moment of my life is for that purpose."

Self-Reflection

Think about your answers to the following questions and then take a few moments to do the exercise. Your answers and actions will help you chart your path of your spiritual journey.

Questions for Meditation:
- ✓ Where am I on my spiritual journey?
- ✓ How does this spiritual journey impact my life?

Exercise: Chart Your Course

We are all on a spiritual journey, whether we realize it or not. Find out where you are on yours. Take a few moments to re-flect on your life and identify the major turning points or mile markers that impacted you most. Go all the way back to your childhood. Perhaps a mile marker was seeing your baby brother for the first time, the Christmas or Hanukkah you received your first "grown-up" gift, your first crush, your wedding day…any significant event that altered your outlook of life. Identify how these events shaped who you are today, and then determine how who you are today will impact your future.

Element Three:
Family With A Religious Background

About one-eighth of the women believed being raised in fami-lies with religion was a significant part of their lives and an important, pivotal element that helped form their spirituality.

Annette, a fifty-two-year-old insurance counselor, clearly told me how important her religious upbringing was. "It [my religion] has always been there when I needed it. It's my strength. A lot of people miss that upbringing in their lives. I don't know how they find their spirituality when they are twenty-one or thirty if they never had it when they were ten and eleven."

Victoria, a teacher, mother, and wife, reflected back on her childhood and warmly told me how people in the religious life interacted in her family's everyday life. "Since I was a child, religion was very strong with my family. It was everything in our social lives. The nuns from our grade school would walk down the neighborhood street and come to our home many times to talk and have coffee with my mother and aunts. When we were baptized and had our First Communion, the priest was always invited to our home afterwards for dinner. It was so engrained in our everyday lives, our origin, our community. Now, it's part of me naturally."

From the snow-capped mountains of Colorado, Jan had also spoken about how important her religious background was to her. "My background is very evangelical in terms of going to a Christian college and studying the Bible in a setting that is very structured in what to believe in and what not to believe in. It was pivotal in the formation of my spirituality."

A forty-eight-year-old woman from Chicago who grew up as a Catholic in a very troubled household explained how her spirituality carried her through the tough times. "Spirituality explained why things happened in my life. It explained the un-explainable."

Self-Reflection

Think about your answers to the following questions and then take a few moments to do the exercise. Your answers and actions will help you understand the role religion plays in your spirituality.

Questions for Meditation:

- ✓ What role did religion play in my childhood?
- ✓ How did my childhood beliefs carry over into my adulthood?

✓ In what ways do my childhood beliefs differ from
   my adult beliefs?
✓ In what ways are they the same?

Exercise: It's Never Too Late

If your upbringing did not include formal religious education, or
if you've strayed from your religious background and feel that
your are off track, realize that it's never too late to start your
spiritual quest. As long as you start the journey, don't worry
about the timeframe. Take some time to learn about various
religions. Which appeal to you? Which do not? Begin meeting
with people in your current church or a prospective church to
discuss your beliefs and how that religion will foster your spiritual growth.

Element Four:
Reaching Out To People & Mankind

Eleven women felt their interactions with people, along with
their sharing and caring with mankind, was the essential element that influenced their spiritual lives.

Donna from Stone Mountain Georgia clearly resounded
this message, "I always try to do unto others what I would like
done to me."

Sixty-nine-year-old Irma warmly told me, "I love people
and have such a heart for children. But peace comes from
within when one loves someone. As the Lord said, 'Love thine
enemy.' If I do that, I have peace."

From Atlanta, Georgia, Barbara, an office administrator,
simply stated, "A key element is giving out to the Universe and
doing things to benefit other people."

Forty-one-year-old Kerry from Colorado also explained to
me, "First and foremost, people are the most important thing. I
feel a true goodness that reaches out and I really can help
people. You become into the likeness of God."

For thirty-seven-year-old Kay from Atlanta, Georgia, it was
seeing people perform good deeds for others that helped her
with her spirituality. She then added a few questions for us to

ponder: "We are here for eighty or ninety years. What's after that? What's the eternity?"

Self-Reflection

Think about your answers to the following questions and then take a few moments to do the exercise. Your answers and actions will help you understand your spirituality through your connections with others.

Questions for Meditation:

✓ Do I consider myself a "people person"? Why or why not?
✓ In what ways do I reach out to others?
✓ In what ways to other people reach out to me?

Exercise: Make Connections

Connecting with others is a simple task. Unfortunately, so many times people neglect to do it. They frequently become pre-occupied and wrapped up in their own world that they forget the small things that make people feel special. Go out today and simply smile and say "hello" to a stranger. Watch his or her face light up. When you acknowledge people, you form a spiritual connection. Other small things you can do include shaking hands with someone, helping an elderly person up the stairs, or offering food to a homeless person. All these are simple things that can have a profound impact.

If you want to touch the world on a broader scale, volunteer in a community organization or devote some time to missionary work. Find ways to reach out to the world so you can share your gifts with others.

Element Five:
Life Experiences, Trials, and Tribulations

A group of the women believed that their life experiences, trials, and tribulations were very difficult elements that forced them to focus on their spirituality.

Forty-six-year-old Marilyn spoke within that context when she said, "The times that have been most spiritual for me have been when there has been some big stress in my life, like when I got divorced and when I lost a dear gentleman friend I was dating. He died suddenly. Life left me really thrown for a loop."

Fifty-year-old Ruth echoed the same message, "There have been so many hard trials and tribulations in my life that made me go back to God and ask Him for help. He has always been the support that I have had and received."

Julianne from Evergreen, Colorado vocalized to me that it was learning through her life's mistakes that enhanced her spirituality. She said, "It [my spirituality] is just what I have been through in my life, the mistakes I have made. The lessons I learned from them have made me realize just what life is all about."

Violet, who has passed away since her interview, told me about her life: "I am sixty-seven years old. I experienced a certain number of things where I had to look for strength. I was widowed at the age of twenty-eight with two young children. My husband died suddenly of a heart attack at the age of thirty-four. I have been a practicing Christian all of my life and I found a great deal of comfort in my religion, especially at that time of my life. I found the strength to know what I had to do, and then I had to go ahead and do it. I had my work cut out for me, because I had two children to raise. That feeling of knowing helped me find the strength to do what I had to do. Continually it was there. It was a source for me."

God bless you, Violet! It was a pleasure knowing you.

Self-Reflection

Think about your answers to the following questions and then take a few moments to do the exercise. Your answers and actions will help you determine how your past trials and tribulations shaped your spirituality.

Questions for Meditation:

- ✓ How did my spirituality get me through a challenging time?
- ✓ How do I access my spirituality during a rough time?
- ✓ Have I ever turned away from my spirituality during a trying time? What happened as a result?

Exercise: Work Through the Tough Times

We each react to trials and tribulations differently. Think back to your most recent challenge. Recall how you got through it. What did you do or tell yourself to make the challenge easier? Now, think of a friend or loved one who recently went through a challenge. Recall what you witnessed him or her do to sustain through the trying time. Notice what you did the same and what you did differently. Use this comparison to develop a sense of respect for what other people go through and how they react to challenges. Use these insights when dealing with future challenges.

Element Six: Basic Beliefs & Faith

Some of the women felt that their faith and basic tenets were the elemental cornerstones for their spirituality.

Thirty-seven-year-old Christine told me, "I am driven by my faith. I am aware of it now more than ever before."

Forty-five-year-old Nancy from Chicago colorfully vocalized, "I am spiritual because I have some very basic tenets that I hold absolutely in the color of violet – they are qualities and ethics that are absolutely care-like. It's a few preciously held beliefs that influence all that I do and am."

Self-Reflection

Think about your answers to the following questions and then take a few moments to do the exercise. Your answers and actions will help you understand how your basic beliefs and faith shape your spirituality.

Questions for Meditation:

- ✓ What are my basic beliefs and faith?
- ✓ Where did I learn these beliefs and faith?
- ✓ How do my beliefs and my faith impact my daily life?

Exercise: Challenge Your Beliefs

Make a list of all the beliefs that are important to you. Then, analyze each one to make sure it really is your true belief and not something you've been programmed to believe. As you reflect on each belief, push all the outside influences out of your mind and look at the belief from every possible angle and scenario. Is this a belief you would cling to even if your life were on the line? Be receptive to the answers you find inside, as they may shock you. Have the courage to ask the questions and to hear the answers. Let the inner voice inside guide you to which beliefs truly are yours.

Element Seven:
Wonders of the World & Universe

A few of the women felt that their connection with the universe and the wonders of the world was a very significant element that helped form their spiritual dimensions.

As Zenaida, who was volunteering as a missionary in Guatemala, told me, "I just feel that given all the wonders of the world and beauty of life, there must be somebody beyond me. One more powerful, omnipotent, and loving."

For Mary, an educator, wife, and mother, this element triggered a lot of philosophical questions. "I think a lot about life and its meaning. Why we are here? Where we are going? Not just for myself personally but the world in general. How do we get here? Why do we die?"

Self-Reflection

Think about your answers to the following questions and then take a few moments to do the exercise. Your answers and

actions will help you use nature and other world wonders to access your spirituality.

Questions for Meditation:

- ✓ How do I use nature or other wonders of the world to connect with my spirituality?
- ✓ How can I make more time for "nature observations" in my schedule?

Exercise: Get Out and See the World

Schedule a "nature break" this week. Take some time to get out of the city or your neighborhood and visit a tranquil place, whether it be a beach, a lake, a forest, or even a beautiful garden. Find a spot where you can be completely alone. Spend some time at that place and just look at the water, the flowers, the animals, or whatever elements of nature are around you. Look beyond any man-made structures and take in the wonder of God's creations. Assess how you fit into the big picture of the Universe.

Element Eight: Life

A few of the women told me that their reverence for life and the pure joy of living was the special element to their spiritual formation.

Valorie, a retired waitress from Albany, Oregon, resounded this message when she said, "What forms my spirituality? Just the love of life!"

Self-Reflection

Think about your answers to the following questions and then take a few moments to do the exercise. Your answers and actions will help you see the connection between joy and spirituality.

Questions for Meditation:

- ✓ What activities bring me joy?
- ✓ How can I do the activity more often?
- ✓ How much more spiritual do I feel when I'm joyful?

Exercise: Spread the Joy

People who love life give off a special aura that showcases their joy. They make others feel good, and people want to be around them. Find a person who gives off this "love of life" aura. Spend some time with him or her. What is it that makes this person so full of joy? What can you learn from this person and apply to your own life?

As we have just discovered, various elements have formed and will continue to form our spirituality throughout our lives. The combinations for the various elements can be as different or as similar as we are. The most important idea for us to contemplate is that we women need to be aware of our spirituality and not be afraid of it. Seek it out. Grow with it.

Each of us is on a spiritual journey whether we realize it or not. Although at times in our lives we might be on a different rung of the ladder from each other, we are not alone. When we bind together as women with the Universe we become like a kaleidoscope. We can only imagine the beautiful pictures we can collectively create.

Chapter Six

How a Woman Learns About Spirituality

"It's almost like a treasure search; I can see God's fingers all over it."
                                                                    Toney

How do women learn about spirituality? Think back and recall the first time you learned about God, angels, and heaven. Were you a child? Did you learn in your mother's arms as she rocked you to sleep and told you stories about Jesus and your guardian angel?

Or were you a teenager? Did you learn about spirituality with your best friends when you stayed up to the wee hours of the night talking and solving all the world's problems? Or was it at a friend's home when her family said prayers before meals?

Or were you an adult? Did you learn about spirituality by picking up a spiritual book in a cozy bookstore? Or did you have a causal chat with a dear friend over a cup of coffee or tea? Or with a co-worker over lunch? Or through a support group?

Are your memories coming back to you? I thought they would. The women's responses to this question, just like yours, are precious. They are our spiritual beginnings, our most cherished and sentimental moments in our spiritual lives. This is when we learned to first crawl, then walk, and finally fly.

Such self-reflection is important because our past experiences are so much a part of our present. They're our base – our foundation – and our childhood represents the most precious time of our lives. Regardless of our spiritual upbringing, we all receive subtle spiritual messages that stay with us and give us a childlike explanation of the world. Those messages ultimately become intertwined with our adult thinking.

These past learning experiences straighten out our spiritual paths. As we move forward, question, struggle, and grow in our spiritual lives, our beginnings are what we frequently refer back to for grounding and clarity. They give us inspiration and strength to move confidently forward on the correct path.

I was blessed to have two wonderful parents who displayed their spirituality in their everyday words and actions. For example, whenever my mother faced a trying time, she would proclaim, "God will help me through this." She always gave it to Him first. As I got older, that mindset stayed with me.

My father, too, was a spiritual person. But rather than use words to show his spirituality, he lived it through his actions. He believed in "living right" and helping those in need. Our neighbors and my relatives knew they could always count on my dad. He gave to his community and family willingly and openly, and he showed a deep respect for everyone he encountered. So between my mother's words and my father's actions, I unknowingly lived the essence of spirituality every day.

"How Did You Learn About Spirituality?"

As I asked this question, many times the woman's eyes would swell up with tears, and at other times pure joy and laughter would radiate from her face as the woman told me about her personal experiences.

Fifty-three of the women clearly stated that they learned about spirituality in their homes when they were children. They recalled that their homes were a warm and special environment that fostered spiritual growth, whether it was through attending Sunday church as a family, reading the Bible together, or learning to face life's challenges through spiritual eyes.

Susan, a forty-five-year-old Chicagoan, said, "Spirituality was taught to me as a child in my home environment. My family taught me about Judaism, about who I was and what I was, and to be proud of that. All of what I am is because of my family."

Regina warmly told me, "When I was little my mother used to read the Bible to us on Christmas evening instead of Christmas stories. And at Easter she would read the whole story of the Psalms to us."

Virginia, who grew up in Southern Illinois, simply told me, "I learned about spirituality through my faith as a child. I lived in a coal mining town, and my family had very little monetary things." For Virginia's family, spirituality was more important than material possessions.

Nancy stirred up memories of old-fashioned Sundays when she said, "My spirituality is so much a part of me. It began when I was a child. My sister and I would always go to Sunday church with my parents. I can still smell the roast lamb or pork cooking when we all came home from Church."

A forty-eight-year-old Yankton Sioux woman described her learning experience. "My grandmother and my grandfather, who was a medicine man, instilled into us traditional Indian values that incorporated the Catholic religion. They taught us that we were all children of God and to view the whole world as spiritual. We didn't dissect spirituality. It was never one word for us. They taught us that God is everywhere. He is everything. The Spiritual Power."

Twenty-seven-year-old Sally learned about spirituality from her friend's household. "My best friend in high school came from a very religious family. We used to talk for hours about spirituality."

Divna explained the difficulties her family had with practicing religion in their home country. "When I was a child, I grew up in a communist country that was against families believing in God and going to church. Fortunately, I was baptized in the Eastern Orthodox religion, and my parents celebrated all the holidays in our own home, as most of the people did in Yugoslavia. However, we could never discuss it openly because the government prohibited it. When someone is telling your family you can't do something, you become quite anxious. That is one of the biggest reasons I came to the United States."

Thirty-four of the women explained that they learned about spirituality on their own, through living and experiencing all of what life had to offer them. Whether they grew up in a spiritual environment or not, they took their own steps to discovering their spiritual path. They just knew!

As Mari Lee simply said, "Just like everybody else, I had to learn through hard knocks."

A thirty-year-old woman from Colorado also told me that she learned about spirituality by living through life's struggles. "I got divorced, remarried, and then shortly after that my baby was born premature with a lot of complications. That was a heavy, heavy time in my life and when I realized there was more to everything. That's when I learned."

Forty-six-year-old Susan told me that her learning started later in her life when "I began to think of myself as a woman and about woman issues; then my learning began."

Ginny, from the northwestern suburbs of Illinois, described her spiritual beginnings in the present tense by saying, "I am living it!"

Liz, an investment wholesaler, prescribes to a saying, "When a student is ready, the teacher will come." She explained, "I think that situations show up for me when I am ready to learn. For example, I went into a bookstore and all of the books were on top of the bookshelf, but there was one book turned around facing me. This book was telling me to pull it off the shelf. It was a very spiritual guide that helped me a lot. This happens to me a lot in bookstores. There will be a book on display that will have my name on it. Or a person will come into my life as a facilitator for me to grow through. Another plan of spirituality!"

Then there was Cindy, who from the beginning of her life had clarity about spirituality: "Since I was a child, I just knew there was spirituality. I came in with my own knowledge as a child."

Ellin also echoed the same. "I had an innate recognition and understanding. I can remember being in a church bus with my church group at a young age, younger than ten. I was talking about life everlasting and talking about the nature of God,

His infinite quality, and the size of the earth compared to the solar system and to the galaxies."

Then there were eight women who learned about spirituality through the formal environment of their church or school, which was always warm and loving to them.

Rose emotionally told me that as a child, after her mother had died, holy ladies of her church brought her up. "I listened and received guidance from everyone, whether it was the deacon or the mothers who were the older ladies of my church. I took their advice. I also read the Bible and learned to believe what was in my heart."

Mary Beth told me that she also grew up in her church. "I was brought up with it since I was a child. I remember going to our church camp and having a bonfire at the end of the week. We all sat around the bonfire and made a confession of faith. We then went in front of the elders and told them that we wanted to become a member of the Church. It was a spiritual commitment."

A forty-one-year-old mother and teacher said the recognition of her spirituality happened in college. "It was through the Newman Center because there were young priests who we could relate to. We were all going through the sixties. We were going to right the world and the hated establishment. But those priests were with it. They kept us on target. It was easy for us in college to not go to church and to turn it off, because no parents were there. The Newman Center was good at keeping us together."

A thirty-eight-year-old woman explained that she also learned through a formal environment, "by going to Al-Anon group meetings."

Quite a few of the women vocalized that they learned by reading soul catching books on the subject of spirituality, and in addition, by listening and talking to people about the subject.

A thirty-nine-year-old woman from Chicago stated, "I learn a lot from listening, talking to other people, and reading a book like 'The Seat of the Soul' by Gary Zukov. That is the direction I would like to be headed in, connecting with the soul."

And ninety-one-year-old Mary joyfully told me, "Watching other people, talking with them, and being with them is how I learn about spirituality."

The Soul's Lessons

Our learning experiences occur in many different places. The settings can be formal, such as in our families, churches, and schools; or informal, like reading a spiritual book or simply talking and listening to people. These various places are beautifully guided from above and are specific for the evolution and development of our individual souls. This is where our spiritual beginnings occurred and where we first learned to walk on our spiritual path to God. Our learning experiences are priceless. As Toney, in the beginning quote of this chapter, eloquently said, "It's almost like a treasure search; I can see God's fingers all over it." What better place could we possibly be but in God's hands?

Self-Reflection

Think about your answers to the following questions and then take a few moments to do the exercise. Your answers and actions will help you recognize your early learning experiences.

Questions for Meditation:

- ✓ How did I learn about my spirituality? Was it through words or actions?
- ✓ How did these early learning experiences shape my view of spirituality?
- ✓ How do these early learning experiences impact my life today?

Exercise: Before and After

On a sheet of paper draw a vertical line down the middle. On the left side of the paper, write the title "What I Learned." On the right side of the paper, write the title "What It Means Today." Think back to things you heard or saw while growing up that you gave a spiritual connotation. Was there a special saying your mother always said? Did your father do a particular action that sticks in your mind? Perhaps a grandparent or teacher said or did something memorable. Whatever it is, write it in the left hand column. Now, on the right hand side, write today's significance of each saying or event. Is it something you do or say today? Have you tweaked a particular lesson to suit your current outlook and situation? When you see how your past influences your future, you get a clear indication of your spiritual foundation and a renewed strength to continue your spiritual journey.

Chapter Seven
Our Spiritual Teachers

"You are a beautiful soul. Be willing to share. Be free to give away pieces of yourself, so I can emulate you."

Nancy

Who are our spiritual teachers – those people who taught us about spirituality? Was it a significant female person in our lives? A mother? A grandmother? An aunt? A sister? A friend? A neighbor? Or was it a significant male person who taught us? A father? A grandfather? A husband? A brother? A boyfriend?

In addition to my parents, I also had aunts and a very special nun who were my spiritual teachers. They were all contemporary, modern people who spoke and lived with a strong spiritual base. Their gentle guidance instilled in me a sense of strength and clarity that surfaced later in my life.

Like myself, the women revealed that they had numerous spiritual teachers. Let's hear what they had to say about each of them.

Significant Female Teachers

Seventy-four of the women told me, without hesitation, that they had a very special female person in their lives who taught them about spirituality. Out of the seventy-four women, twenty percent of them were fortunate to have had two significant female teachers. And there were even a few women who were privileged to have had three very special female teachers.

Listed next are the special roles the significant female teachers played in the women's lives and the frequencies with which the women mentioned them. As you look over this list, recall who your significant female teacher was and the special role she played in your life.

Role	Frequency
Mother	50
Grandmother	19
Personal Friend	6
Aunt	4
Teacher	3
Sister	2
Group of Women	2
Nun	2
Mother's Friend	2
Pastor's Wife	1
Spiritual Guru	1
Neighbor	1
Therapist	1
Girl Scout Leader	1

A Woman Like No Other

Fifty women stated that their mother was the most significant female teacher in their lives. Some of their responses included:

"My mother was a woman of substance."

"She led me."

"My mom planted the seed of spirituality for me."

The women repeatedly told me that they learned about spirituality more by watching their mother's actions than by her spoken words. It was how their mothers lived their lives by performing loving and caring actions for them and others. As forty-three-year-old Karen joyfully said, "My mother is my hero! She taught me by example. She didn't talk very much to me about spirituality, but I watched her. Her example has helped me with my daughter. Her example was more important than anything else."

Nancy lovingly echoed the same description about her mother. "I don't think it was so much as Mom teaching me things, as it was in a sense of living and caring that emanated from her. It was how she acted. I don't remember words."

A fifty-five-year-old Chicagoan woman admired her mother for her wonderful caring actions to others. "My mother is out there today as the counselor for the little town in which we live. She takes care of other people. She is very giving. My mother sees service to others as a light in her life."

Fifty-two-year-old Annette emotionally remembered her mom. "My mother was my base for spirituality, by example. She never sat me down and said, 'This is how life is and what it is all about.' She wasn't a written text. It's been thirty-one years since she died. She was a saint."

The Matriarch

Nineteen women said their grandmothers had a tremendous impact on their lives and made sure that they stayed on the straight path to God.

Stephanie clearly stated how important her grandmother's role was to her and how it impacted her entire family's way of living. "Grandma was a very strong and religious woman who had a lot of common sense. We could never gossip at home. If we did, she would tell us to first look at ourselves and take care of our own problems before we start worrying about the next person. We came from a poor neighborhood; there were a lot of problems around us and we could have gone astray. But we didn't because Grandma was there. We had to live right. There was no wrong way. We had to live the right way. That is the way she believed."

A seventy-four-year-old woman warmly explained her grandmother's influence on her. "I learned from my grandmother. We were very close. I didn't particularly realize this at the time, but she was praying for me to go back to church. When I finally went to mass and communion at the cathedral, I wrote her and told her. She was in tears. She told me that she was praying for this all the time. My mother and I were going through a lot of friction, and my grandmother and I were very close. She had a big influence on me."

Twenty-seven-year-old Sally lovingly said, "My grandmother showed me spirituality. She came from the 'old ways' and she definitely instilled a lot of things in my life. We could never say that we didn't want to go to church. Even if we couldn't stay through the whole service, we had to go for a part of it. I used to live with her. She didn't talk a lot about spirituality, but she lived it in the true sense."

One woman simply and proudly remembered her grandmother as "an absolute saint who always talked about Jesus and His love."

Birds of a Feather

Our personal friends are powerful teachers too. They are the ones we talk with, cry with, laugh with, and grow with. When a strong bond of friendship exists between two women, it allows for the spiritual thread to be interwoven between them. This spiritual friendship then becomes a supportive and understanding environment that fosters a woman's learning needs. Every woman who has experienced a spiritual friendship understands this and treasures it. Words cannot describe the impact we have on each other.

A woman from Oregon lovingly talked about her special friend from Stockton, California. "She has been a friend for over thirty years. When I feel I need someone to talk to, she is the one to whom I turn."

Ellin from Colorado talked proudly about her good friend in Chicago. "She would be interesting to interview because she studied spirituality. It was her life quest. She started out as in international model and chose to study life. She has been a significant influence on me, a driving force. She introduced me to an Indian teacher. He was a singer along life's line. He's my greatest teacher. He incorporated spirituality with life."

A thirty-eight-year-old woman explained how her friend turned her life around for her. "After my situation with drugs, I started going to a Unity Church and met a very spiritual woman who invited me into business with her. I was able to leave the brokerage firm, which was an environment that was creating an opportunity for self-destruction. I was then able to be outside with nature to race sailboats, which allowed me to channel my self-destructive behavior into a positive exercising manner. I was able to attract into my life a business partner who is very spiritual. She meditates and does Yoga. She is on the same path as I am. I had to undergo changing my centers of influence and my network. I had to let go of some people in my life who did not support my spirituality in order to make room for those to come into my life who would."

For two women from Colorado, their special aunt was the most significant person who taught them. "Our father's sister took us to Sunday school when our parents weren't taking us. Spirituality was her life."

For one woman, her high school teacher was the one who taught her about spirituality. "She was a significant person in my life. In fact, I named my daughter after her. She taught Catechism in my school. She was a model for me."

And twenty-eight-year-old Martha explained how her art teacher in high school nurtured her spirituality. "She was my spiritual connection. We were both hard on ourselves in the same way, but we had reverse reactions. She was more like a mother to me than my own mother because she sat with me and nurtured who I was."

A thirty-one-year-old nurse and mother said it was, "A group of women that I had worked with. I was having personal problems and felt I was missing something and couldn't figure it out. They helped me understand who I was. One of the women bought me my first Bible study guide. All of us nurses worked the night shift and we were all Christians."

A forty-four-year-old woman from Colorado spoke about her previous experience in a convent and about a special nun who had an impact on her. "There was a nun who was in charge of our formation. She was a very holy person and open to bending the rules. She taught me that what is important is who you are – how you allow God into your life and out into other lives. I still think of her."

In some instances, our mother's friend can also teach us. A social worker and baker repeated that message to me. "My mother's friend is a strong person. Because of the way I grew up, my option was to either maintain a strong feminine Christian perspective or live in rebellion. I didn't know there was anything in between. She was living proof there was an in between."

A thirty-seven-year-old woman from Georgia told a powerful story. "My mother had a woman in her life, Mrs. Brown, who is my mother's guardian angel 'til this day. Her house was catty-corner from ours. She came in and took care of us whenever Mother needed to go somewhere. She taught my mother how to cook, because my grandmother did not want Mom in the kitchen. Mrs. Brown talked to my mom a lot about her life. Even though Grandma and Grandpa talked to Mother a lot, it was Mrs. Brown who came into my mother's life and made a difference. I live by Mrs. Brown's theory of life. My mother was concerned about how to repay Mrs. Brown for her kindness, because we didn't have two nickels to rub together. Mrs. Brown said, 'Down the road someone is going to need you to do something for them. That's how you repay me.'"

Now I would like to share with you a beautiful story of how a loving seventy-five-year-old neighbor brought a little sunshine into a six-year-old girl's world. "I connected with this neighbor when I was six years old. Six particularly stands out in my mind, because six was my time of awareness. I wasn't in a family like other kids because my parents were drinking all the time. My neighbor was a role model. She was seventy-five years old, and she taught me many things, such as life might not be perfect but you make the best of it. She also read poetry to me all the time, and because of her I am a lover of poetry today. She was my role model. I don't think she necessarily prayed. She maybe went to church, but there was something about her. She was blessed. It was very good for me because of the place I was at the time."

Nancy relayed an important message that she definitely wanted us to hear. "I was blessed by a number of people in my life, including teachers and Girl Scout leaders. What is important is the message I received and that I'm trying to give you. Feel free to give the pieces of your soul away."

Thanks, Nancy, because that is exactly what our female teachers have done for us. They shared their magnificent souls with others and with us through love, comfort, inspiration, and joy. They are the significant women in our lives.

Significant Male Teachers

Not all women have female spiritual teachers, and that's perfectly normal. Some women are closer to their father, grandfather, brother, or uncle than to any other family member or friend. When it comes to spirituality, we're all the same. In fact, fifty-six of the women stated that they had a significant male or males in their lives who taught them about their spirituality.

Listed are the special roles the significant male teachers played in the women's lives and the frequencies with which the women mentioned them. Can you identify your significant male teacher from the list and the special role he played in your life?

Role	Frequency
Father	34
Grandfather	5
Friend	5
Husband	4
Uncle	4
Brother	2
Clergy	2
Neighbor	1
Teacher	1
Spiritual Guru	1
Boss	1
Counselor	1

Father Knows Best

Thirty-four women stated that their father was the most significant male teacher in their lives. Kathy from Atlanta, Georgia proudly said, "My dad taught me about spirituality. He is the nicest man I have ever known. I don't think he ever said anything bad about anybody. He is truly a spiritual man. He is an angel."

Yes, our fathers are our angels. That's exactly what my dad was to me, and still today, I miss him dearly. Our fathers give us love, guidance, support, and encouragement. They are our strong spiritual pillars.

The women frequently told me that they learned more about spirituality by watching their father's actions than by his spoken words. Lorraine echoed that by saying, "I saw spirituality in the way my dad treated other people. He was very quiet, so I had to watch real close." Nancy from Birmingham, Alabama said with much pride, "I learned spirituality by his actions, not by words. He was doing for others constantly." Marsha from Indiana explained this further. "Spirituality is not something you can teach from a blackboard or book. It's just there. I watched my dad's movements, his actions, and how he reacted to a situation. He never gave up, just like my mother. Whatever happened, he taught me to move on and learn from life experiences."

A twenty-three-year-old young lady explained how her father kept her path straight during her teen years. "In high school, my dad would say, 'I'm going to tell you what I prefer for you to do. Then you have to make the decision.' He has been an example to me on how to raise my children. The main thing with my father was his honesty in dealing with people. Also, if he made a commitment to someone he always followed through on it."

Kay was very grateful to have a father like hers. "I realized early how blessed I was. All my friends throughout the years seemed to come from families where only a mother raised them, or where one parent was an alcoholic, or where a father would beat their mother, or their parents were divorced. Their fathers were never there for them. Even though my father happened to travel Monday through Friday every week of my life, he was always there for me, whether he was physically present or not."

The Patriarch

Five women lovingly said that their grandfather was the most significant male teacher in their lives. "My grandfather was a very kind and loving man. He taught me to look for kindness in a man and in a relationship," one woman said.

A sixty-six-year-old woman fondly remembered stories told to her about her grandfather. "My mother told me many stories about her life in Poland and how she loved her father. My grandfather was a super religious man. He lived it. He served mass every day until he was seventy-two. He never missed a day. He was a blacksmith and would burn his hands in the fire and have blisters all over them. When he was a twenty-four-year-old man, he was thrown off his horse, tossed into cold water, and then shortly afterwards he started to have epilepsy spells. When he had his epilepsy spells, he was not aware of what was happening to him. My mother was concerned that he would hurt himself or die one day with those fires. He would say, 'God would never let me die that way. I will know when I'm going to die.' And he did. That is the way he was. He lived it."

Mr. Right

Stephanie warmly spoke about her husband as her spiritual teacher. "He seldom gets mad. He is very good with people. He's right there to help people, and that I feel comes from God. God gives this to him so that he is able to do for others."

Susan respectfully talked about her husband because he never hindered her growth as a woman. "My husband never stopped me from doing things. I have talked to other women friends who have said: 'I have to ask my husband to do that.' I never did. I give him the courtesy of letting him know what I'm doing, and we support each other. We have grown spiritually in our lives."

Other Great Men

For a few of the women, their special uncle was the most significant person who taught them. As one woman warmly said, "I thought of him [my uncle] as my second dad. He was always supportive. He was always there and would be willing to take the time. He was just as busy as my father was, but there was a bond, and there still is."

A seventy-four-year-old woman from Chicago also talked about her uncle. "He was a Maryknoll missionary. He used to write to me when I was little. He was a prisoner in Japan and later with Chinese Communism. He had a big impact on me when I was growing up."

Evelyn lovingly told me what an angel her brother was to her and her family. "It was my older brother who took over my father's role when my parents divorced. He was in the military service and made a career out of it. I would hear his name from my mother. She was appreciative of him and loved him so much because of what he was trying to do. He understood how she was trying to make it with eleven children. I could remember him sending checks to my mother and saying to get the kids this and that. I could remember how I wanted roller skates when all the other kids had them, but my mother couldn't afford them. Another time I needed a typewriter for school, but mom couldn't afford it. But I wrote to my brother and I got them!"

A forty-five-year-old woman described the Reverend from her family's church as her significant male teacher. "Reverend Frank had shocking white hair and the most translucent skin I have ever seen. He had a sense of peace within himself. I could tell that he was proud by the way he carried himself. He was truly quite a different individual. He was physically centered, therefore physically commanding. I liked that."

A thirty-one-year-old woman from Colorado warmly spoke about her neighbor and his wife. "They were probably the most unique people I have ever met in my life. He was a published author who wrote a lot of articles for the newspaper. He was a very kind and gentle man."

One woman said that her boss was her spiritual teacher. "It was odd. I got pieces of my spirituality from him. He gave me a book that got me thinking in a different direction."

A forty-six-year-old woman from Chicago talked about her counselor and friend. "He was a counselor, but I knew him as a male friend. He was the one who really helped me recognize how unhappy I was. I would say things and he would ask, 'Did you hear what you just said?' I think he came along at the right point in my life. I didn't get divorced because he was in my life. I got divorced because he helped me recognize what was wrong in my life."

No Significant Female or Male Teachers

Sixteen out of the one hundred women who were interviewed said there was no significant female or male teacher in their lives. As one woman clearly said, "There was no one as far as guiding me in that direction. It has been totally on my own." This was echoed by another woman, "I would have to say I did this all by myself."

Traversing the spiritual path alone takes courage. We need to commend these women.

This particular interview question evoked many memories and emotions in the hearts and souls of the women interviewed. It was quite evident that the significant teachers in the women's lives made a strong impact on the women's spirituality. Their teachers emanated exemplary qualities, which inspired the women to incorporate those qualities into their lives and for some to alter the patterns of their lives.

A special spiritual bond developed between the women and their teachers, which lasts today, whether their teachers are alive or are in the spiritual realm. Their souls had touched each other for a moment in time. Their teachers' spiritual messages remain with the women and will throughout their lives.

Self-Reflection

Think about your answers to the following questions and then take a few moments to do the exercise. Your answers and

actions will help you identify your spiritual teachers and their impact on your life.

Questions for Meditation:

- ✓ Who was my significant spiritual teacher?
- ✓ What lessons did I learn from her or him?
- ✓ How does this person (or his or her memory) impact my life today?

Exercise: A Word of Thanks

Think about your most influential spiritual teacher. Picture that person in your mind. Now, get a sheet of paper and a pen and write a letter to that person stating how he or she impacted your life. Detail the specific lessons you learned from the person and how those lessons shaped who you are today. Conclude your letter by thanking that person for his or her guidance. If the person is still living (and if you have the courage), mail the letter to him or her.

Chapter Eight
How a Woman's Spirituality Develops

"Spirituality evolves when one experiences it. It is not a stage. It is a process." **Zenaida**

How does a woman's spirituality develop? The answer is from the very first time we women hear about God, heaven, and angels to the time we can clearly state that spirituality is a significant part of our lives.

What happens during this process? What helps us move from A to Z spiritually? Can we describe our spiritual processes, the different ways that God speaks to us?

During the women's individual interviews, I requested each woman to reflect back on her life and identify specific ways in which her spirituality developed. After one woman answered this question, she looked at me straight in the eyes and astonishingly said, "Michelle, it was like looking back and seeing how short I was!"

Collectively, the women were able to describe five general processes to their spiritual development, the special ways that God had reached their souls. They are:

- As a woman grows and matures.
- Through life's trials, tribulations, and joys.
- Through observation and interaction with people.
- By reading, studying, praying, and meditating.
- Just accidental.

Each of the one hundred women, at the time of their interviews, had experienced anywhere from one to as many as all five of these processes in their lives.

Take a few moments to reflect back on our own life. Identify the various ways that God has spoken to you so that you can discover how far you have truly grown in your own spirituality and how you can continue to keep soaring forward and upward on your journey to God.

Personally, I can identify with each of the processes the women spoke about. And by looking back over my life and identifying these events and processes, I can see how far I've grown spiritually, as well how far I still need to go. I find it a very positive experience as I recall what I've overcome and as I envision what I can yet become.

Let's examine each of these processes in detail.

As a Woman Grows and Matures

Fifty-eight of the women clearly told me that their spirituality developed simultaneously as they were maturing physically, mentally, and emotionally. It was a progression that occurred from their childhood through their womanhood, whether the women were consciously or unconsciously aware of it.

As an education public relations woman from Missouri simply stated, "My spirituality just kept growing as I grew as a person."

A forty-year-old teacher and mother explained that her spirituality developed as she grew mentally and intellectually. "Actually, my spirituality was something that evolved and went on. When talking about different levels, I came from the level of a child who believed what knowledge was given to me from my Sunday school teacher to learning about my own spirituality. As one's intellect evolves, one's spirituality also evolves."

A thirty-nine-year-old registered nurse described her spiritual development as it actively progressed through her various life cycles in a short and easy to understand narrative. "As a child, I thought God was in the sky watching over us. Then as I became older and learned how to read, I tried to integrate

Biblical stories that God is good versus evil with the connotation and that God is watching over us. After that, my spirituality became prevalent in the sense of community, which came from the organized religion to which I belong. It helped me connect to God. I attended religious programs, instructions, group discussions, lectures, and so on, expanding my religious knowledge base. I have been doing this for two years and will continue doing this. I learned about spirituality as a child and then it progressed through my life cycle."

A forty-six-year-old mother, wife, and administrator for leadership ministries and corporate leadership development reminisced and identified her spiritual life "as a map." She said, "One thing leads to another. The earliest time was learning from my mother. I had extra pressure being single and being in a culture of the sixties that was going crazy, while maintaining a morality from a culture that was rapidly disappearing. Then I had marital pressures and was not happy. Not having my marriage be what I wanted in my mind did not make it easy. Another was having a child, because my son accepted the Lord when he was quite young. Now he's through college. It hasn't been easy. It's been difficult, but grand!"

An executive secretary to a vice-president of a large U.S. firm explained how her anger was a driving force that brought her back onto her spiritual journey to God. "My spirituality started as a child with my family. I received something out of grade school and high school. But my anger was the biggest catalyst to get me back to spirituality. I wanted to prove it."

A thirty-six-year-old registered nurse described her spiritual development more as a philosophical progression throughout her life. "It happens in stages. I go to one step and was with one truth for a while. Then after I was in that truth for a while, I was led to another truth. I just progressed that way."

Twenty-one out of the fifty-eight women identified specific growing stages or certain times in their lives that were pivotal to their spiritual advancement. These included grade school, high school, college, and specific chronological ages or times in their lives, such as in their twenties and forties or in the nineteen-sixties.

For an eighty-seven-year-old retired woman and house-wife, "It was through eighth grade at my parochial school. We were taught about spirituality every day through Bible and Catechism classes. That has stayed with me. It has never left me."

A forty-one-year-old dental hygienist and single parent had also spoken about eighth grade as a significant time for her. "The real turning point was my confirmation in eighth grade when I joined the church. This is when I realized there was a difference and there was spirituality."

Thought-provoking reflections in high school about life's blessings was the catalyst for a forty-four-year-old administrator of school age childcare programs and training. "I started thinking about spirituality and that I was given so much. I know it wasn't just for me, but I was given it to share. I still feel that today."

A forty-three-year-old mother, secretary, and word processor extraordinaire, as she described herself, concurred by saying that her spirituality had also developed in her high school years, though in her case it was with the help of a very loving and playful grandmother. "When I was in high school my grandmother and I set on this project that we were going to read the Bible every night devoutly. We agreed to sit and read at least two chapters every night. I remember we went through these words we couldn't pronounce. We would get hysterical because we couldn't figure out if we said the wrong name what would happen if we did. We would laugh and keep on reading. Then the next night before we started reading the Bible again, we would talk about what we had read about the night before."

College years were instrumental for a fifty-year-old woman in the advertising field. "As a child I knew spirituality was there. But I didn't know who I was until I was a college student and then converted to Judaism."

Attending a public city university had a strong impact on a twenty-nine-year-old registered nurse's spiritual development. "When I was little, it was the neighborhood that I grew up in that helped me spiritually. Then I went to a public city university and I was able to see people from all different aspects of life, whereas before my high school was predominantly Irish Catholic."

A forty-seven-year-old-technical skill librarian recalled a particular time from her early twenties. "I think the first time I ever thought about spirituality was between my junior and senior years in college, when my world had just been expanded and opened. My sister, who was two years younger, and I spent the summer between my junior and senior years in college talking about the philosophical events of life and what we called our 'metaphysical discussions.'"

A forty-three-year-old nursing administrator joyfully told me about her spiritual discovery in her college years. "It really jelled when I went to college. I didn't learn about a specific religion, but about other religions of the world. I discovered that I had learned some basic beliefs from my family and they were also the foundations of the religions I was learning about in college. Once I got to that point, I solidified everything."

The journey to spirituality began in the sixties for a forty-one-year-old executive director of a non-profit regional center. "For me it was very much attached to my religious orientation. In college during the sixties, I took a lot of religious courses. It certainly was interesting exploring Christianity and understanding theology. That was my beginning. Also during college, we all had to deal with the Vietnam War and the questions we were asking collectively as well as individually. Then I went into neutral for many years. Three years ago, I was describing to a friend how I wanted more depth, and we talked about it. We decided to go through the process of studying and understanding the method in terms of meditation."

A thirty-seven-year-old woman emotionally told how troubled times influenced her spirituality. "It was during the late sixties and early seventies, when I went through a lot of drugs, soul searching, and searching for the meaning of life. In that time I found a lot of different things that I tapped into. I lived it."

A sixty-year-old bookkeeper, mother, and grandmother identified her twenties as a significant spiritual time for her. "I was twenty-two and started a full-time job. I had a lot of time at night and no outside interests. I started working at the rectory in the evening and helping the priest perform odd jobs. That is where I got close to the clergy and started developing."

For another woman it was in her thirties. "I started paying attention in my thirties and not much before that. Certain things just started connecting. Meeting you. Meeting certain other people, talking, and just getting more. I guess it was time to happen. It was just timing."

Self-Reflection

Think about your answers to the following questions and then take a few moments to do the exercise. Your answers and actions will help you identify critical points in your spiritual journey.

Questions for Meditation:

✓ During what life stage or at what age did I start to develop spiritually?
✓ What happened during this time that triggered my spiritual development?
✓ What specifically did I learn during this time?

Exercise: Your Life's Timeline

Get a sheet of paper and position it so the widest area is horizontal. Draw a line across the page. At the far left hand side, write the word "birth." On the far right hand side, write the word "present." This is your life's timeline from birth to now. On the timeline, indicate the significant events that you recall in chronological order. Think as far back as you can, and write down everything that comes to mind, no matter how insignificant it may seem. When complete, examine the events you recalled. Which ones occurred during your spiritual development phase? What events led up to that phase? Focus on that life stage to get a true picture of where you were emotionally and spiritually so you can better understand your spiritual growth cycle.

Through Life's Trials, Tribulations, and Joys

A significant number of women explained that various trials, tribulations, and joys were the significant catalysts in their spiritual development. So many of us can easily identify with these women, because we have all experienced some trial or tribulation and joy in our own lives.

For many of us, trials and tribulations are the most trying parts of our spiritual journeys to God. And they are definitely the most profound learning and growing experiences in our entire spiritual lives. How else can some of us hear what God is saying to us? Would there have been spiritual growth for us without such challenges?

Then there are the joys – the beautiful, beautiful joys in our lives. They are the strong loving affirmations of spirituality in our lives and the manifestations of God's magnificent love for each and every one of us. Our joys are our little bits of heaven on earth. Let's hear the women explain this significant developmental process in their lives.

A fifty-year-old senior vice-president of residential sales simply and wisely said, "The trials and tribulations teach me – the cause and effect. The problems happen. I pray for help. I ask for help. It comes."

A forty-one-year-old mother, homemaker, and food program consultant explained that spirituality was "really hard." She said, "I think it's tested every time I make a choice, even if it's a simple choice. For example, do I take these paper clips home or do I leave them here?"

A forty-eight-year-old woman emotionally described her difficult life story to me. "I came into the world unprepared. I had to stumble around and go through a lot of trials and tribulations and errors. In 1974 I found a different way of living. I call it the hell of my life because I learned about everything: smoking, drinking, social services, and jails. Finally, I came out of that and went to an alcoholic treatment center and recovered my spiritual part."

A thirty-eight-year-old woman sadly told me about her childhood, "As a child, my life was not right. I lost my mom when I was six years old. My father was an alcoholic, and I was shuffled back and forth [between relatives' home]. Events weren't the ideal I dreamed of, even as a child. But I knew I was a good person. Now as I look back, I realize it was then that my spirituality developed. I didn't recognize it then, but it made things okay."

As one very aware woman encouragingly said, "We all develop spirituality in our lives by the experiences we go through. But we don't all accept it, acknowledge it, or become aware of it. It is by becoming aware of it and wanting to grow with it that you turn into a spiritual person. I think our experiences in life and whether we were going to allow it to be a positive influence on our spirit is a matter of choice. It all boils down to truth work."

Then there was a thirty-year old saleswoman, wife, and mother who joyfully told me, "I was always very happy with everything that has happened to me. I've never been unhappy at any time in my life. I look positively at life. I feel so lucky. Many times I get down on my knees and thank Him for giving me such a great life."

Self-Reflection

Think about your answers to the following questions and then take a few moments to do the exercise. Your answers and actions will help you see how your trials, tribulations, and joys, affect your spirituality.

Questions for Meditation:
   ✓ How have my life's trials, tribulations, and joys affected my spirituality?
   ✓ What particular event, either positive or negative, helped me develop spiritually?
   ✓ What did I learn from the event?

Exercise: A Continued Timeline

Go back to the timeline you previously created. Look at the events that you wrote down. Next to each, indicate if the event was positive or negative at the time. Looking back, do you still consider the event the same way, or has your outlook changed about the event? Are you now able to see the good that came out of it, if any? Why or why not?

Through Observation and Interaction with People

A few of the women described how their spirituality developed through other people – by talking with them, by closely watching how other people handle and cope with life, or by having a heart-felt discussion with a close friend or a group of friends. As one woman simply and clearly stated, "I get a certain intrinsic goodness about people from the get-go."

A twenty-eight-year-old waitress and artist explained how her spirituality developed during her yoga classes. "It was quite powerful. It was good. There were five other women. It was my first experience where women were supportive to each other and cared about each other."

A forty-eight-year-old manager said, "I think it was just part of my life and the people I met. I was fortunate to meet very good people – people who were very positive and who had a positive effect on my life."

A forty-seven-year-old director of a Head Start Program for children services explained: "Spirituality became visual to me and very real because I could see people who were walking in spirituality. It was making a difference."

A forty-six-year-old nurse researcher and coordinator of quality assurance warmly explained, "It comes from my children – from being around them and watching them grow up."

Then there was a darling story from a seventy-four-year-old semi-retired woman who reminisced about a young boy and his family during World War II. "When I went overseas during World War II with the Red Cross, I met a boy there and he was Catholic. He didn't try to apostate. Just seeing him and his family, that religion meant a lot to them, was so important. I was impressed by the way they lived."

Self-Reflection

Think about your answers to the following questions and then take a few moments to do the exercise. Your answers and actions will help you understand how other people's actions influence your spirituality.

Questions for Meditation:

✓ How do I interact with people on a daily basis? (i.e. – take a self-improvement class, go to community meetings, etc.)

✓ How do these interactions with others impact my spiritual journey?

✓ How can I get involved with more people so I can expand my circle of influence?

Exercise: Develop a Spiritual Circle

Look in your community newspaper for the "Events" section. This is the section that details upcoming events, club meetings, support groups, and other community involvement activities. Choose one upcoming activity or group meeting that appeals to you. Maybe it's a women's club meeting or a charity fundraiser. Whatever you choose, schedule the event or meeting in your day planner, and go to it. Talk to as many people as possible while there so you can make new acquaintances and develop some community and personal bonds. When you expand your circle of influence, you open the doors for greater spiritual growth.

By Reading, Studying, Praying, and Meditating

A few of the women explained how reading, studying, praying, and meditating had strongly impacted their spiritual development. Does this sound familiar to you? Maybe it happened to you through a soul catching spiritual book that was a gift from a dear friend. Or was it an angel book that was just sitting on the shelf and tugging at your soul to read it? Or was it studying that most remarkable book, the Holy Bible?

Spiritual books are thought provoking, challenging, and very powerful for our souls. They allow God to inspire us through the written word. They clearly teach us how to move forward and upward on our journeys to Him.

A thirty-year-old woman explained how a special book was pivotal to her spiritual pursuit, especially after growing up in an atheist family. "I read a book about the Blessed Virgin Mary. She is the one that brought me into the Catholic Church. I didn't know Jesus, but I knew Mary. I had read so much about her. Now I'm learning a lot more about Jesus. If it weren't for her, I wouldn't be in Catholicism right now."

Studying and reading about religious people, such as saints, was instrumental for a Midwest police officer. "My spirituality developed through the nuns who taught me about the lives of the saints. To me, the saints were powerful. The nuns were trying to show us that saints were ordinary people like you and me. That gave me a sense of spirituality. I tried to emulate the lives of the saints. When I had library hour at school, I always picked books about the lives of the saints, and I still do today."

A thirty-year-old investment broker said, "One thing I feel is that we are all shown spirituality in our lives, but we need to find out about it. I am an incessant reader. I find most of my information from reading books. It would become quite apparent to me what I should learn about. They would be shown to me in books, articles, signs, posters, or flyers."

When we pray or meditate, we acquire the sense of God's presence. We can never underestimate the impact that these sacred actions have on our spiritual lives. They are the most powerful moments we experience. This is where we receive our inner strength. As a thirty-seven-year-old business owner, wife, and mother peacefully said, "I pray. I go into my soul. I honestly pour out my feelings over to the One and the Only."

Wow! Just you and God.

Self-Reflection

Think about your answers to the following questions and then take a few moments to do the exercise. Your answers and

actions will help you assess how reading, studying, and meditating contribute to your spirituality.

Questions for Meditation:

✓ How often to I spend quiet time alone sorting out my thoughts and feelings?

✓ What can I do to make more time for reading, studying, and meditation?

✓ What have I learned during times of spiritual reading, studying, and meditation.

Exercise: Take Time for You

Schedule fifteen minutes a day for reading, prayer, or meditation. During those fifteen minutes, turn off your cell phone and stop everything you are doing. Use that time to read from a spiritual book, to say a quiet prayer, or to get out and walk in nature. Devoting just a few moments each day to yourself and your spiritual well being helps you triumph over any daily challenges.

Just Accidental

Only two of the women stated that their spiritual development occurred by accident.

A thirty-nine-year-old workshop coordinator and mother told me her story. "My journey was haphazard. It almost seems accidental to me. I went from one job to the next, which led to another, which led me going to massage school. Massage school led me to breaking my arm, which led me to getting my current job. I never doubt when something happens whether it's for a reason. I feel like I have been led. I always see that there are patterns. So, I think it is karma in some ways."

A thirty-one-year-old mother and registered nurse explained, "By accident – totally by accident. It's almost like I said I had a need and I didn't know what it was. God had three angels, R., J., and J. We were all working that night in the hospital and it was funny, because we were actually arguing. They said, 'Just read the Bible. Just read it.' They pushed me to just read it. They said, 'Just do this and realize this is what is missing in your life.' They were strong."

Spiritual development is a process that takes time. We cannot rush it. We must live it and experience it deeply. Do not underestimate its importance. As Violet simply and eloquently said, "Spirituality develops almost of itself, once you realize the importance of it."

Self-Reflection

Think about your answers to the following questions and then take a few moments to do the exercise. Your answers and actions will help you see how the seemingly accidental things guide your spirituality.

Questions for Meditation:

- ✓ Have I ever felt God's hand in my life? What happened?
- ✓ When have things in my life seemed to have "happened for a reason"?
- ✓ What were the outcomes of these events?
- ✓ How did the outcomes affect my spirituality?

Exercise: Chaos by Design

Describe an event from your life or a loved one's life where something seemed to "just happen." How did the event affect you or your loved one? Looking back, was the event truly "accidental," or did things seem to work out for a reason? Detail specifically what happened and pull out any themes you notice. Use this information to give you perspective as you continue on your spiritual journey.

Chapter Nine
The Organized Religion Connection

> *"Organized religion is like a tool that I feel. It is food for my soul."* **Sarah**

Seventy-five out of the one hundred women who were interviewed told me, without hesitation, that they practiced their spirituality through an organized religion. "It gives me a model, a way of living my faith, my belief," one woman said. "It gives me a purpose," another echoed.

Only fifteen of the women responded with a definite "no." As one woman told me, "My organized religion just did not allow for free thinking."

Ten women explained that they sometimes practiced their spirituality through their organized religion, but it was not in a consistent manner. Notably, seventy of the women clearly stated that their organized religion helped them connect with their spirituality. Mary, from Lowell, Indiana, stated that it was an absolute necessity: "If it wasn't for organized religion, I wouldn't have my spirituality."

Bonnie, a twenty-nine-year-old account service representative, further explained to me: "Organized religion is the only way to get what is inside of me and the height that I am at the moment. It is the knowledge that I have the ability to keep going up." A thirty-nine-year-old woman from Chicago stated that her organized religion pointed her "in different ways that I would not have been able to see in my life. It fosters personal growth. It teaches me."

Terry, a thirty-nine-year-old registered nurse, pointed out the importance of organized religion's Christian teachings. "It enhances my spirituality. The Christianity teaching and the mystery involved always make me constantly search because of Jesus Christ being the concept of Christianity."

From Colorado, a forty-four-year-old woman explained how previously living in an organized religion convent had liberated her spiritual thinking and made her realize that spirituality was real. "I had been a nun for eleven years, and that experience liberated me. When I left the convent I remember my sister asking, 'Who was in the convent? You or me?' From that perspective of being a nun, spirituality became real. It wasn't legalities. It wasn't you are a Catholic so therefore you have to do such and such. It opened my mind. It opened me up!"

Thirty-eight-year-old Sandra had a delightful perspective on this whole subject matter. "My religion keeps reinforcing to me that God is there. He cares about us. He looks after us. We are not alone. He is somebody we can all call on when we're in need. We are looking this way and He is up there looking down, and He has a much better perspective than we do. He sees what is all around us, whereas we only see with blinders on."

Several women indicated that organized religion was a support system to their individual spirituality and gave them "the strength to live and cope with life." A thirty-year-old-investment wholesaler from Atlanta, Georgia vocalized this by saying, "I feel that I receive support and inspiration. It [organized religion] helps keep me in touch. Organized religion is really a support system for individual spirituality." Another woman concurred that her organized religion was a support system for her spirituality: "The support is in the form of discussions. We talk about everyday situations. We share facts and ideas and make it a support group."

A significant group of women strongly felt that it was their particular religion that helped them connect strongly with their spirituality and God. With some of the women, it might not have been inclusive of every ritual or belief of their religion, but a certain sacred intricate part of their religion that helped ignite their spirituality. It could have been through their religious practices and rituals, or through their church's heavenly atmosphere, or the loving, sensitive priest or preacher who inspired and comforted them through his sermon. Let me share with you some of the women's comments about their religions.

Baptist:

- "My church is unique as most black churches are. They want us there no matter how we look or the way we are dressed. They don't want us to use any excuse to not come to church. They want to be able to fellowship with us and help us with any problems that we are going through."

- "When I go to church the preacher welcomes me and I feel so good."

Born-again Christian:

- "It's where I can be fed and inspired on a weekly basis. I become part of the Body of Christ, which is the church universal."

- "I found Jesus like I never knew Him before. We dance in the spirit."

Church of Christ:

- "The classes at Church help me grow and that's where my spiritual growth comes from. Iron sharpens iron. Man sharpens man. Our minister also gives us many foods for thought in our group services. The worship services are not the minister giving to us, but an interaction with each other, the singing, the praying, and the giving."

Dutch Reform:

- "I don't feel comfortable in other churches. I've tried. I don't know what it is about my own church. I guess it's the people I grew up with there."

Eastern Orthodox:

- "The whole atmosphere makes it easier for me to connect with the universe."

Judaism:
- "I can talk to God. Pray to Him. I feel God is indirectly looking over me."

Lutheran:
- "The organized worship within the church environment makes me more aware. The spiritual aspect is always there."

Methodist:
- "My church seems to be more for the people. They don't pressure us. There are a lot of group classes and I attend the Bible study class."

Mormon:
- "Not all of their beliefs, but their teachings that you are children of God."

Native American Indian:
- "I go to an Indian chapel where the priest adopts Cheyenne and Roman Catholic ways. I feel comfortable there. We are taught there is just one God and He belongs to all of us."
- "It is the ritual of the Native American Indian concepts. Connecting with your higher self and a shared relationship with everything in the universe and that you are an integrated segment."
- "The shield journey, which goes on for a year and is guided by an Iroquois healing woman, is important. I ritual all year long in cleansing times of activities. At the end of the summer, I will build a shield that is the consequence of all those things I have done throughout the year."

Non-denominational:
- "It is daily and weekly. When I go to church, I come out with new wisdom of how to be a better person."

- "I hear a sermon that gives me strength to pull myself together more so I can say there is a purpose on earth."

Pentecostal:

- "By studying the scriptures. My church is not the building, but the people you connect and share with."

Protestant, non-denominational:

- "We have a real dynamic worship service."

Presbyterian:

- "Today, the sermon was wonderful. It included the Lenten explanation of the meaning of the Cross."
- "My religion, my church, and my Bible studies keep me focused, as does getting together with people who have the same beliefs."

Roman Catholic:

- "The rituals of the Catholic Church are grounding."
- "Going to Mass with other people and reading and studying theology has made a tremendous difference."
- "It gave me a structure on what the ideal life should be."

Siddha Yoga:

- "Through meditation. It has to do with the aspect of knowing God and knowing oneself. The water is the same. Yoga is interested in the water."

Unitarian Universal:

- "It helps me connect with people who have the same ideas. It is a very liberal religion that has been around since the fifteen hundreds. Some of the early founders of our Constitution built our beliefs of freedom of religion, color, and race into our early American history."

- "When I go to church, I get a chance to reflect on things."

Unity:
- "It gives me the freedom to be myself. There is no judgment involved with the Unity Church. They are so aware of what God is and what life is all about."

What's interesting is that although the religions are different, the women echo the same themes. So even though the beliefs may be different, the way people experience religion and spirituality is the same.

When Organized Religion is Missing

Fifteen women felt that organized religion did not help them connect with their spirituality.

"Organized religion has formed my base, but I am now away from the rules they set down. I see it from a broader spectrum. I don't have to go to church to fulfill my obligations. It is with me all the time. God is with me wherever I go. I don't have to go to church because it is Sunday. It is something I practice every day, not one day out of the week," said a forty-six-year-old Chicago woman.

From Denver, Colorado a forty-year-old-woman explained: "I prefer a spiritual practice with a group of eight couples which is more exploratory [than organized religion]. Some of the couples are educators and intellectuals who studied religions around the world. We talk with each other about the nature of what is happening in our lives and support each other. We find peace, comfort, and strength. We support each other in maintaining virtues that are generally associated with spiritual discipline around the world."

A few of the fifteen women said that they were actively searching for spirituality in their lives. Here is what they had to say:

"I'm searching right now to see what makes me comfortable. I don't believe in rituals or organizations when it comes to spirituality. I believe that it is a very personal thing and that everybody needs to find what it is that can make them contribute to the world," said Barbara.

A thirty-seven-year-old woman from Atlanta, Georgia explained that she "used to practice." She continued: "I've gotten away from my particular church. I want to get back to an organized religion and I need to find another church to connect with my spirituality. The one church I was going to was too large and too impersonal. I need to get back to a smaller church – a more close-knit one. I am trying to find another religion to connect with. I want to go to prayer meetings again."

There was a consensus among these fifteen women who were not definitely sure if organized religion had really helped them connect with their spirituality. As one woman said, "Well, it does help, but it doesn't. There are parts of it that are so rigid and so judgmental and I don't want to connect with that part. Then there is another part of quietness and an inner faith and a confidence. It's so hard. It's really a combination at this point."

"In a way it does [help me connect] and in a way it just comes from within me. I feel I don't have to look at somebody else to get to the Maker. I go to the Maker on my own. It has to come from within," said Rose from Chicago.

Another woman concurred: "Sometimes I feel that going to Mass and to church brings me closer to God. Sometimes I don't always get what I need out of it. It could be because I am so wrapped up in my daily life."

Jackie, a Chicago woman, explained that she goes to church and believes it is a good thing; however, "I don't feel you have to go to church. When I feel the need I go inside and connect with Him. It is in my heart. It is more in my heart than in religion. My temple is my heart."

The Path Back

Two women were seriously considering returning back to the traditional practices of organized religion because of their concerns for their children's spiritual development. A twenty-nine-year-old mother, wife, and supervisor vocalized her concerns. "Right now I've fallen and I'm trying to get back because of my two-year-old daughter. Organized religion was always in my home. When my family comes down here we go to church. I guess I don't realize it, but my spirituality comes from somewhere."

A thirty-year-old mother, wife, and saleswoman echoed the same. "I'm more lapsed now. We are going back to church because we have the baby and we are trying to do more of the traditional. A lot of it is through prayers. I go to church by myself to think. Quiet times. I get my head together and think about God."

Life crises seemed to cloud the importance of practicing through an organized religion for some of the women, and therefore caused them to put their religion on hold. In some cases, it was a complete halt to practicing their organized religion.

A sixty-year-old-woman sadly told me, "After my husband died, so many things happened to me. I couldn't understand why I was hit with such big disasters. It wasn't only his death at age fifty-six, but also the things that happened to me after his death. I'm seriously thinking of going back to church."

A twenty-six-year-old woman heartbreakingly told me, "I do not practice through my religion since my mother died about four years ago. I think I am still hurting. "

My Journey

When I questioned the one hundred women about their opinions on organized religion, I found myself reflecting back on my life and how organized religion had impacted my spirituality. I realized that I was very fortunate to have been brought up by two warm and loving parents who had devoutly practiced their spirituality through organized religion. They demonstrated to me that spirituality was very real and part of everyday life. Therefore, because of my parents, organized religion was very much part of my entire childhood and part of my high school years.

However, then came the sixties and I foolishly placed my religion on the back burner. I did not, at that time, see religion and spirituality as high priorities in my life. Instead, I slowly and very subtly placed my spirituality out of my reach and out of my sight. I did such a fine job with this maneuver that I almost lost my spirituality completely. Then I started to experience life's trials and tribulations, which thank God, forced me to realize that something was definitely missing in my life. I wasn't sure at the time what the missing piece was, but I definitely knew it was vital for my soul. That's when I started to spiritually search.

I incessantly read every book on the subject of the spiritual and metaphysical dimension that I could get my hands on. I read about different religions, their beliefs, about near death experiences, reincarnation, karma, and creative visualization. I attended various lectures and seminars and listened to renowned experts on the subject of spirituality. All of this brought an eclectic amount of ideas and concepts to my soul. But still, something was vitally missing: the real soul connection. But what was it? Would I ever find it?

I then started to go back to church, the Catholic Church, the organized religion that I grew up with, the one that taught me how to pray, how to talk to God, and how to listen to Him. Without being consciously aware of it, my spirituality desperately needed to be grounded in religious traditions. My soul had yearned to go back home, and it did. I had finally discovered the missing piece.

Because of my own deep spiritual search through the years, I have become extremely open and sensitive to other women who are on their spiritual journeys and searching for God. Therefore, this is not an authoritative book about organized religion. It is about the individual spiritual journeys of women and how we struggle with our spirituality, how we live it, how we experience the heavenly joys, and how we inspire others.

The wonderment of it all is that as we move forward and upward on our own spiritual paths, we will find other souls like ours – other women from the sisterhood of women who will share part of the journey with us and give us support, encouragement, and guidance. So keep your hearts and souls open. Be receptive to God when He sends a helping hand to bring you home.

Self-Reflection

Think about your answers to the following questions and then take a few moments to do the exercise. Your answers and actions will help you see how organized religion plays a part in your spirituality.

Questions for Meditation:

- ✓ What role has organized religion played in my life?
- ✓ How do I derive my spirituality from organized religion?
- ✓ If organized religion is not important to me, what activities are that get me closer to my spirituality?

Exercise: How Do I Connect with God?

What specific act do you do, or what specific things do you say, that help you connect with God? Are your words or actions tied to a particular religious ceremony or belief? Investigate the basic tenets of various religions to see if your own connection path with God can be seen in other religions as well. Once you discover how alike various religious beliefs and customs are, you can communicate with people on a more spiritual level.

Chapter Ten
The Impact of Work Experiences

"My work challenges my spirituality. To live the way God wants me to live. To be loving. To be giving."

Kate

D o a woman's work experiences have an impact on her spirituality? On her soul? After a good day's or night's work, do we feel a little better inside because we helped make life a little easier for someone? Maybe that is the reason we choose our occupations or professions, because we want to help others and make a difference in the world.

Could our work be our true vocation in our life? Or is it just a job in which we are counting the hours, day after day, waiting to retire?

Work is something we spend most of our lives doing, whether it is in our homes or outside of our homes in various work environments. And we often find ourselves spending more time working than we do living our personal lives. After all, who else will buy the groceries, drive the children to school, or take our elderly parents to their doctor's appointment? Who will pay the mortgage, the children's dental bills, or our elderly parents' medical expenses?

Spiritual balance and inner harmony are so vital for us as women. But how do we women maintain a spiritual balance in our demanding and hectic work environments? Maybe we never thought it was possible or even realistic to think about our work and our spirituality in the same context. Therefore, I was curious to hear the one hundred women answer the question about their work experiences.

I was pleasantly surprised to hear that seventy-four out of the one hundred women clearly stated that their work experiences had a definite impact on their spirituality. They considered their work experiences to be special spiritual paths that helped them fulfill their soul's purpose on earth.

In my own life, my profession as a nurse is very much a part of my spirituality. Ever since I was a little girl I wanted to be a nurse, and by working in a profession of caring and helping I have had the opportunity to impact people's lives every day. Even today, since moving away from patient care and getting involved in hospital administration, I relate to others with the same compassion and understanding that I had done with my patients. So for me, my work certainly is an extension of who I am – of my spirituality.

Now let's hear the women describe how their work experiences involve their spirituality.

The Business Field

Investment Wholesaler:
> "I am in a male dominated investment business. It has created the opportunity for me to look at my own identity and my own spirituality. If I don't have a strong sense of who I am and the essence of my being, it could be a very threatening situation. I love men and I appreciate them. It would be easy for me to take a different track. It makes it very comfortable for me to be very feminine. In a male profession some women have a tendency to become a man rather than accentuate the positive, which is their own femininity."

Marketing Coordinator:
> "A couple of the companies I worked for tested me a lot as to my honesty and my integrity. They taught me that I could be honest and still survive. I had bosses who would say, 'Just tell them I'm not here.' I would

say to them, 'If you want me to tell them that you are not here, then you walk outside. I'm not going to lie for you! I just won't do it.' This has helped build on my spirituality."

Saleswoman:

"I deal with people a lot. My job also gives me time to be alone in the car. Sometimes I'll just drive and I won't even have the radio on – total silence – and I'll think about the day, about what's happening, and about the good things that are going on."

The Healthcare Field

Pediatrician:

"I think it is the chicken and egg theory. I do what I do because I love people. I really believe it's important to make a difference, to teach, to help, and to be. I can't imagine any other profession that would allow me to do this in the manner in which I am doing it."

Psychologist:

"Yes, it's worship, working with people who are suffering mentally. Helping them define the meaning of suffering and self is directing them in their lives. Their soul development."

Hospital Administrator and Registered Nurse:

"I became a nurse because my inner spirituality unconsciously led me to it."

Registered Nurse:

"I am connected to the caring, faith, and strength. The wonderment. Children with adopted parents. Even mothers who had to make the decision to give their children up for adoption. I always saw a message of love."

Registered Nurse:

"It's just the simple fact of caring for people. A patient voices to me, 'The Lord will see me through this surgery.' It allows me to talk to them. They are in such a fragile time! Their faith is all they have to hold on to, if they have that."

Registered Nurse:

"Nursing is a service to people. Look at somebody who's a burn victim. The patient really stinks in a burn ward. The thoughts in my mind were, 'How could I ever really take care of them? What allows me to care for this patient?' My thoughts then become, 'If you do this for the least of my creatures, you do it to Me!' In this burn patient, He allows me to do things that I couldn't ordinarily do."

Registered Nurse:

"I always did like working with the elderly. They can teach us something. We can help them, because most of the time they end up in a nursing home and need someone to care for them. I felt that was the place I wanted to be and make things better. I think nursing is one place where one's spirituality is strengthened by one's experiences. Nurses deal with life and death every day, whether they want to or not. Some of the things we see and some of the human interactions just eat your heart out. These things we see strengthen spirituality."

Registered Nurse:

"I have been a nurse only seven years. We deal with people in a compromised situation where they are dependent on us. Their lives are different when they are in the hospital, even if it is a minor thing. They have lost some control over what they can do and what they can't do. I am able to give them something to help them get through, and sometimes, they in return give me something. I don't think there is any other profession in the world where you impact on so many lives across so many cultures and boundaries as you do as a nurse. When I took my maternal-child rotation and studied all the things a woman's body goes through and how it adjusts to this creation of a new life, I think, 'How could someone not believe in God or higher power?' I still cry at deliveries. A life! A person! A human being! It breathes and thinks and has its own soul."

Pediatric Emergency Room Registered Nurse:
"I see such tragic things happen so quickly. I can see the spirituality come out as parents pray to God to save their children. I work with these children and know sometimes that the work we do in the emergency room wasn't because we did it; it was above and beyond what we could do to save a person. It was God himself who pulled these kids through. In no occupation other than religion could you see different connotations of God and spirituality."

Nurse Recruiter and Pediatric Registered Nurse:
"Nursing strengthens my spirituality. It is one reason why I do extra shifts. It's when I practice nursing on the patient care floors that I can do that little extra. Anybody could go in and inject antibiotics into I.V. solutions and change dressings, but not anyone can just stand there and talk to parents and go the extra mile. Tell them where they can make referrals. Because of my bad circumstances (a mother of a child profoundly retarded from birth), I try to make it a little easier for someone else. I don't want anyone to have doors shut in their faces, like I had. No one knows the cruelty I went through. I don't want anyone to go through it if I can help it. If I could make that difference for them, I'll do it."

<u>Social Worker:</u>

"I am working with a large community in Washington,
D.C. who are handicapped adults. The men are handicapped and are unable to hide their brokenness as well
as we can. It is definitely a spiritual experience."

The Educational Field

<u>Learning Disabilities Teacher:</u>

"This field I'm in does [contribute to my spirituality],
because these little children have flaws. God gave them
to the earth with flaws. I see them doing things and I
can't help but believe in God. They can't count and
then they finally can. They can't add and finally they
can add. They can't read and they finally can read.
When I say flaws, I don't mean to be negative. God
didn't give them everything they were supposed to
have, that everybody else has, yet they make it! I know
there has to be a God to do that. God wouldn't put
them on earth unless there is a reason for them to be
here. It is so neat when they come to me and give me
a big hug and kiss. I think this field has a lot to do with
spirituality."

<u>Educator, Teacher, and Facilitator:</u>

"I work in inner city schools. These kids are terribly
deprived. There is every type of abuse, deprivation,
poverty, teen pregnancy, drugs, and learning problems.
Everything! It's hard. It's challenging. I've stayed there
for twenty-four years because my spiritual self is there.
If I can get a child to learn a single sound of the alpha-
bet, graduate from high school, or not be a pregnant
teenager, I did this one thing. This thing was God. I
have to look at the little things and not the big picture.
So I have to look for little miracles. Try little, tiny ones."

Spanish Teacher:

"Every day I walk into class and I pray over the students silently to myself. Every child there is someone's child. The things that happen are fantastic. I see miracles in my classroom all the time. It's not me. It's God!"

Junior College Educational Counselor:

"I am a counselor and coordinator for the young Native American Indian students coming into college. I can practice what I preach. I had three women come in who were older and had nothing. They had no education, and they wanted to better themselves. They came here to get their GED degree. Now one is on her way to Berkeley, California, and the other two are in their second semester in junior college. I feel good about myself knowing that I was instrumental in their lives. I have to have motivation. They were surprised. They underestimated themselves. They had no faith in themselves."

Teacher:

"Share the wealth. Share the gift. Share the peace. Pass it on. Build up that other person. I was a school teacher for seventeen years."

Junior College Teacher:

"I don't receive much money, but I fulfill a need. If I can get one child's life to turn around, it's all worth it. There is more to life than we are living."

Teacher:

"I'm in the position, as a teacher, to deal with adults who come to my classes. I attract seekers, people who are seeking certain things that are fun in their lives and who are ready to change. It's not that I'm changing them. I just happen to say something. I'm a catalyst."

Judicial and Criminal Field

Police Officer:
> "I treat people like I would like to be treated. I try to bring God into my work as much as I can to help people, especially victims. People feel so frustrated and don't know where to turn. I try to give them help, shelters, and places they can go for help. A lot of these people are homeless, lonely, and battered. They are victims of oppression. I would like to do more of it in my work, especially for victims, people who have lost a loved one due to natural causes, violent crimes, or suicides. It's tough."

The Child Care Field

Executive Director:
> "My work is a mirror I made – a mechanism to begin to look at who this person is and to me. It's happening through work."

The Metaphysical Field

Astrologer:
> "Every day is a bigger reward than the one before. It is absolutely amazing, especially in the beginning when I didn't know if I was really reaching people. Now they are all waiting in line. I never thought about what I was telling them. People would come back and quote what I said to them and tell me what happened. Half the people interpret it and get a message they need to hear through me. It reaches them. That's what I care about."

The Service Field

Service Manager:
> "Because I deal with people, and there are so many different people with different personalities, I have to remember to go within myself and think. How do I want to be treated? How would I feel if this happened to me?"

Retired Waitress:
> "Interactions with different groups of people give one a lot of insight on what people are like and what their experiences are. I learn a lot through their experiences, even if I haven't really been through them."

Concierge:
> "My satisfaction is doing different things for other people and trying to make their lives a little easier. That is my part as a human being for the universe, which makes me have peace and a good night."

The Secretarial Field

Executive Secretary:
> "My work challenges me to live what God wants me to do: To be loving and to be giving. It also challenges me to grow in other areas of my life."

Secretary:
> "Yes, responsibility helps me to grow."

Secretary and Cashier:
> "I keep my standards high. I wouldn't do anything that I didn't think was right. I relate that even to customers. They never see me frowning. When I get home, then I let down."

The Creative Field

Artist:

"I produce sculpture plant forms that are very organic and very female. Very often it is the motif of push and pull. There is a balance between male and female components. What is the balance? How can I work through? A lot of the forms I view as very rigid and tight, then I concentrate on opening up, so that individuals could help each other, affirm each other in connectedness."

The Traditional Roles

Homemaker and Mother:

"I was a homemaker. My spirituality was through my children. I feel sorry for mothers today, especially working mothers. They have to work so hard to bring home a hundred and a quarter."

Mother:

"It is just one more relationship, and that relationship was brought about by the Divine Being and made all powerful."

Mother:

"I tell my children all the time how grateful I am for them. I realize what life really is because of them. I look at them. There is this little baby. I know they are people and they think and they create life. The life we have created will create other lives. They will pass the torch on."

When It Doesn't Match

Twenty-six of the women explained that their work experiences did not have a definite impact on their spirituality. Here are their work experiences.

The Business Field

Operations Manager for Real Estate Company:

"No! In fact, I have to really concentrate on being centered in the work environment with certain people. I enjoy my job, but when I am on a day-to-day basis with people who do not practice spirituality or are not aware of their spirituality, I struggle with them."

Designer/Trainer for Software Company:

"I would say it works completely against it, unfortunately, because of the things that happen at work through and in my company. There are a lot of power struggles – the typical big company things that I think are all the opposite of Christianity and the beliefs behind it. So I go on autopilot and I try not to let things bug me. I try not to get involved in it, although it's difficult not to do. When I leave the building I can physically feel a change come over me, because now I can say, 'Okay, I'm walking away from that.' I know that it's not the basis of who I am, and now I can relax a lot more. "

Account Service Representative:

"No, I think it is a testing ground."

Real Estate Saleswoman:

"In real estate you can do some real crappy things and make a good living. There is a wide variation of behavior in this business that you won't go to jail for. It's really a question of how to conduct yourself. I was talking to a good friend of mine in Virginia who was saying that in these times, more than any other times, you have to have your own personal integrity about things, because everything else is falling apart and there are no absolutes. So, you sort of have to be your own spiritual warrior out there. Do your own thing to the best of your ability and according to your own life."

The Healthcare Field

Nurse:
"Spirituality helps me as a person. I think there is a distinct difference between spirituality and my growth as a person. Spirituality helps my work, but I think you could do nursing without being spiritual."

Clinical Social Worker:
"I feel a little bit jaded by my work. There are really great things that happen and some really beautiful things that the kids or their parents say and do. Then there are some horrible things that happen and real losses that we all experience."

The Educational Field

Teacher:
"I'm the token, the only Jewish person in my work establishment. I'm an American. I'm a woman. My religion is Judaism. It was very difficult. They gave me a hard time."

School Social Worker:
"My work experience is so crazy that I don't think so."

Filling the Void

As we have just read, it can be very difficult and trying for women, who are aware of their spiritual dimensions, to work long hours in environments that are not conducive to their spiritual growth. It forces them to place their spirituality on autopilot while they are working. Some of the women, however, found solutions to their dilemma and chose to utilize their free time as a means to filling their spiritual voids. As Pope John Paul II eloquently said on Mother's Day, May 5, 1991 at an open air mass in the Barriers Stadium of Portugal, "Free time regains the humanizing dimension which work loses." (Chicago Tribune, May 13, 1991, Section I, Nation/ World, page 5.)

So that is what a few of the women did. They filled the spiritual voids in their work lives by actively participating in volunteer work outside of their normal work schedules. Here are their stories.

Director of Finance:

"The volunteer work I do through the school keeps me in touch with my spirituality. I've been working with cocaine-addicted babies. It just touches the spirit of the child and that makes me more aware of my own soul."

Technical Skills Librarian:

"For the past five years I have been teaching a black woman how to read. By doing that, I think it has brought out some of the values that I have in terms of dealing with other people and patience. She has given a lot to me, as I to her. So I suppose, with all of the work I have done, it's more my volunteer thing that probably has come the closest to using my human skills."

Executive Director of Child Care Services:

"One summer when I was in college I worked in a hospital in Chicago and I was a good friend of the head nurse. I was able to see a baby born, surgery, and a person dying. To really see birth, life, and death I felt the reality of the cycle of life and that was very spiritual."

One woman, a registered nurse, clearly stated that she had experienced spirituality in her daily work environment, but had decided to also go some very special extra miles. Here is her wonderful story about her spiritual adventure. "I am a lay missionary in the Dominican Republic. I'm a member of the health team there. We give consultations to patients. Sometimes we have to walk, and we can't go far. We see the patients over there, and after medically consulting with them we provide them with medication. At the same time we do training programs for the health care workers in the different communities. It is very satisfying. Most important, my experience allows me to reflect a little bit more on the spiritual life. My prayer life is enriched."

Our work, wherever it may be, in our homes or outside of our homes, on the farm or in the city, whether it is volunteer work or a paid salary, is our spiritual path that helps us fulfill our soul's purpose on earth. It does not matter how diverse our work experiences may be from each other, for we all can experience soul growth. Just look close to your soul. It will lead and guide you to where you are going.

It is remarkable what we women will do to honor our souls and others. Through our actions, we can make a difference. By doing so, we bring a little bit of heaven on earth to others. Bravo!

Self-Reflection

Think about your answers to the following questions and then take a few moments to do the exercise. Your answers and actions will help you see the connection between your work and your spirituality.

Questions for Meditation:

- ✓ How did I choose my current profession?
- ✓ Does my work bring me closer to my spirituality? How or how not?
- ✓ What kind of work-related activities can I bring into my day that will contribute to my spirituality, whether they are paid positions or not?

Exercise: If I Could Be Anything – Find Your Soul's Purpose

To discover your life's calling, imagine that you have all the money you need to live comfortably. You're retired from your work and have enough money to support you and your family for the rest of your life. With your days free, what would you do to fill your time? What activity would you pursue? What would make you happy? What would you do for free? Your answer is your life's purpose. If your current profession is not in alignment with this vision, what can you do to bring some aspects of your purpose into your day?

Chapter Eleven

Shifts of Consciousness to Spiritual Awareness

"It reawakened in me what had been dormant for many years."
Ellen

Have you ever experienced an incident in your life, or in the life of a loved one, that had such an impact on your soul that your viewpoint on life and the world changed from that moment on? Perhaps the incident touched the depth of your heart and soul and awakened your spirit.

Whether the incident was positive or negative, such as the birth of a child or the death of a loved one, it undoubtedly touched your soul in some way. That's because these moments cause us to stop and evaluate our lives as well as our future goals. Through these events we learn to identify what is really important to us.

Personally, the moments that affected me the most were the death of my father and the onset of diabetes. Both of these moments reinforced for me the frailty of life and the preciousness of health. They each brought me closer to my spiritual roots and my internal journey.

Do most women experience these shifts of consciousness that allow them to expand in their spirituality? If so, which significant incidents in their lives cause such spiritual shifts of consciousness? Would the one hundred women want to share their personal experiences with me?

Ninety-eight of the one hundred women stated that they had definitely experienced incidents in their lives, or in the life of a loved one, that had resulted in a heightened awareness and an expansion of their spirituality. The women further explained that their experiences had a profound impact on their souls and had caused dramatic spiritual changes in their lives. This question brought forth many personal memories and emotions from the women.

Collectively, the women had experienced over one hundred and fifty significant incidents in their lives that had definitely challenged and expanded their spirituality. I wish I could share with you, in detail, all of the women's stories, but that would be a book in itself. However, I have listed all of the women's significant incidents, along with their frequencies, for you. As you read over the list of significant incidents, you may recognize some of the same incidents in your own life, once again proving that you are not alone. We are each walking with other women who are on their spiritual journeys to God.

Significant Incident	**Frequency**
Illness/Trauma/Death	
Death of someone close to them	27
Personal illness	12
Illness of someone close to them	9
Drug and alcohol abuse	4
Trauma of someone close to them	3
Abuse by relative or significant other	2
Near death accident	1
Suicide attempt	1
Marriage/Relationships	
Divorce	13
Marital problems	6
Parents divorce	5
Breakup of a major relationship	4
New marriage	3
Meeting husband	2
Marrying spouse with a different religion	1

Significant Incident	**Frequency**

Motherhood/Children

Experiencing childbirth	4
Being a mother	3
Adopting a child	2
Through children	1
Daughter violently raped	1
Daughter in prison	1
Son in war	1
Son being baptized	1
New family of husband	1

Religious Issues

Religious experiences	3
Changing/joining different religion	3
Spiritual services/ceremonies	3
Spiritual retreat	1
Mother changing religion	1
Studying how people relate to different religions	1
Meeting a spiritual teacher	1

Life Cycles

College	4
Adolescence/late teens	3
Childhood	2
Grade school	1
Late twenties	1
Graduate school	1
Getting older	1
Massage school	1
Jungian psychology school	1
The 1960's	1
Assassination of President John F. Kennedy	1
World War II experience	1

Significant Incident	Frequency
Personal Changes	
Own questioning	6
Geographical move	4
Job change	3
Joining a support group and therapy	3
Starting own business	1
Financial crisis	1
Work experience	1
Bad choices	1
First orgasm	1
Left convent	1
Left Indian reservation	1

Heavenly Happenings

Fourteen out of the one hundred women explained to me that they had experienced special incidents in their lives. I refer to them as "heavenly happenings," because they came from above and from the Divine. I include them here because they are indeed the most profound. Here are their stories:

"One day I was sleeping. I had a dream about the Blessed Virgin Mary at Medjugorje. I was unfamiliar with Medjugorje. When I woke up I was thinking about it. I thought, 'I must have read an article about this somewhere.' So I had a bunch of *Newsweek* magazines and I went through every single one. I went through probably fifty copies looking for this article, because I thought I had read it, but I couldn't find it. It was an obsession for two days. Finally, I mentioned it to my roommate, and she said, 'You know, I happen to have a book on Medjugorje, which I have never read. It's in my closet. I bought it at a garage sale. Let me get it for you.' So she gave it to me. I read it. As soon as I read the book I believed. I knew that this is where

I belong." (Converted to Catholicism after being raised as an atheist.)

"I was dreaming that I had a fever and I was in this whiteness. A voice came out of the whiteness and I saw the face of Christ. He said, 'It's time now,' and He handed me a cross. The cross was extremely beautiful with many jewels. I said, 'Oh, you don't want to give that me, Lord. I might drop it.' Then, out of the whiteness, I picked up the cross. That was the beginning of my spiritual experiences and connecting to God."

"One night when I was ten years old, I was in my bed and I went out of my body. I went up out of the earth and through the stars. I could look back and see a cluster of stars that formed this shape. It was a human shape made up of stars and galaxies. It was almost an experience in my dream of seeing God. Being a teeny weenie speck in the body of God that was similarly shaped like me. I remember talking about this to the rest of my friends. They got very upset because it was scary. I guess it was the way I was talking about it. I remembered that the teacher and minister had reprimanded me for talking about this. I stopped communicating my inner experiences at that point. Much later I discovered people who understood the spirit, in that fashion, and didn't have the same kind of boundaries that most religions have now."

"I would have deja vu experiences with palpitations and cold sweats. I would chalk it up, because I came from a scientific background. I remember an incident that had occurred in college and I was very upset, so I talked to my mother about it. I found out that my grandmother had also had deja vu experiences, and they had also scared her a great deal. It is something one has, a genetic type of spirituality".

"I am a hemophiliac carrier. When I had my hysterectomy, I ended up with complications. I was in the hospital and had lost a lot of blood. There was one experience I remember. I was going into shock. My blood pressure was dropping. My pulse was rising. They were throwing hot blankets on me. I was in complete panic state. I was focused on how I had to get through this ordeal. I thought there was a chance I could die. I didn't want to die! All I remembered was my father (deceased). I prayed to my Dad, 'Please pray for me and watch over this.' And I prayed to God. I said, 'I don't want to go. I don't want to leave my family behind. But if I have to go, just be with me. Forgive me for my sins.' All of a sudden there was a blonde nurse taking my pulse. She's holding my hand. Everybody is around me, doing what he or she has to do, preparing me to enter surgery again. It's one o'clock in the morning and this person is standing there, telling me it's going to be okay. She calmed me down. I felt such peace. I looked up and thought, 'God brought you here for me. You are here for me.' She helped me. I do believe she was an angel! The following day, I asked the nurses who she was. There was no explanation. I told them her name, and they replied, 'There is no nurse on this floor by that name. We don't know whom you are speaking of.' But she held my hand up till we got to the operating room doors. Then she let go. Then I knew everything was going to be okay."

"My husband, who I had only been married to for six and one-half years, died. Months later, there were a lot of questions that had to be answered. I experienced something very unusual. I was sitting alone in the living room. All kinds of thoughts were wondering through my head. I don't know if I dozed off or what, but I had the feeling that there was a presence in the room. I heard the words, 'Don't worry.' A great sense of peace came over me. I knew what I had to do and I did it. It was just one of those things. I think it was my Lord. I had no problem with that. I have not told this to many people, because there are a lot of people who would not understand it. I think I mentioned it once to a preacher. He accepted it. People do experience things like this!"

The women have spoken.

Self-Reflection

Think about your answers to the following questions and then take a few moments to do the exercise. Your answers and actions will help you see how life events impact your spirituality.

Questions for Meditation:

✓ What significant events do I recall that changed my spiritual outlook?
✓ Specifically how did my outlook change?
✓ Have I observed others who had an outlook change due to a life event? What happened?

Exercise: Changing Moments

Sit in a quiet place. Think deeply and ask yourself if you've experienced an event in your life that caused you to have a change. Was it a positive experience? Was it a negative experience? Stay with the memory. If it was negative and it causes you pain, allow yourself to cry. If it was positive, then stay with the peace. This is a very personal moment for you. Did it awaken something that was dormant inside you?

Chapter Twelve
How a Woman Expresses Her Spirituality

"Expression of our uniqueness is an offering to God."

Elaine

Is it important for a woman to express her spirituality, to show a part of her soul to others and to the world?

"It's extremely important," said Liz from Georgia. "That is the only way I can make a difference."

Annette further emphasized, "If more people expressed their spirituality, we could have a much better world."

This is how eighty-six women felt about the importance of a woman expressing her spirituality.

Forty-five-year-old Cynthia from Chicago strongly believes that expressing her spirituality is "as important as it is to be, because it may help someone else who is despairing see beyond tomorrow." It is the anchor that she gives to someone, to hold him or her up.

From Missouri, one of the women told me that she didn't mind expressing her spirituality but was not forward with it. "If the occasion arises and I feel it needs some recognition or it will help someone, then I'm very outspoken."

Karen, however, from Quincy, Illinois, said that she has to express her spirituality. She strongly believes if she doesn't share her spirituality, then she shouldn't have it. She presented this little narrative. "The clothes rack doesn't take anything or put anything out; the sponge sops it all in and enjoys it; but the spark takes it in and passes it on! That's what spirituality is all about. If we don't pass it on, why do you have it? I want to be a spark. I want to make a difference. I want to be a light."

Rose from Chicago informed me that she had been through the part of her life where people were ashamed of being spiritual, where they didn't want anybody to know because they might think less of them. "However, when I let my spirituality show, I receive better spiritual stimulation."

Forty-five-year-old Nancy stated, "People aren't feeling good about themselves or what's happening around them. They are not hearing spirituality. People used to know about the importance of expressing spirituality and could just feel it."

Spiritual expression for forty-seven-year-old Ellen is very important, because it is "being human with the highest qualities. Spirituality brings out the best in the human. We all exist on several levels, the physical and the sensual, but if you don't have spiritual quality, what does it matter? I guess it's just a matter of wanting to experience life from the heights to the depths at all times and to live intensely."

Fourteen of the women did not feel that it was very important for them to express their spirituality. As a forty-one-year-old teacher said, "I don't know how important it is to express spirituality to anyone else, but it is important that spirituality is there for me." A forty-year-old wife, mother, and hostess from Indiana echoed this sentiment. "It is more important to have spirituality than to express it."

A fifty-year-old woman simply said, "I'm shy about expressing it." Another woman stated that she did not express her spirituality because "it is an extremely private thing, an enormously restful position. God is restful."

For some of us women, it is easy to express our spirituality. As Cindy from Chicago eloquently said, "I just have to breathe and spirituality flows from me." But for some of us women, it is not easy to express. As Patricia from Wisconsin summarized, "Spiritual expression is with the individual, the person; it may be silent, or expressed in your actions."

We all need the opportunity to express our spirituality because our spirituality is the very essence of who we are. And if we deny our spirituality, we are in a way denying ourselves. If you're afraid to express your spirituality, surround yourself with those who exude spirituality and gain the courage by observing them and taking small steps on your own. You can make a conscious decision to accept your spiritual nature and embrace it.

Spiritual Expressions

Would the women want to share their spiritual expressions with me? Would they be able to describe how they really express their spirituality to others and to themselves? Without hesitation, the women were able to describe many ways in which they expressed spirituality in their lives. First, let me share with you some of their simple and very delightful expressions:

> "When I buy flowers or when I have intimate meals with my friends and we are connecting and talking. It is the essence of my spirituality and so beautiful."

> "It's in the little things that I do, like something I wear, or a book I am reading, or a walk in the woods."

> "My own private meditations, or long walks, or spending weekends by myself."

> "By sharing and writing notes."

> "When I whistle and sing. I sing when I do the dishes."

> "Exercising. Jazz dancing."

> "Through my music."

> "Sometimes through words. Mostly through singing."

> "Creating with my hands."

> "By swirling in the enthusiasm of my life. Listening to the relationships around the earth, the sky, and me. Maintaining a sense of humor."

> "I go to the temple and pray."

"By attending church regularly and saying morning and evening prayers. Talking to the good Lord Himself when I have the need."

Quite a few of the women expressed their spirituality through their relationships with others and felt the inner need to have a helping and supportive impact on others. Here are a few of their special spiritual expressions.

"By showing love whenever I can."

"Giving someone a hug."

"By being positive and happy."

"In my smile and how I talk to people."

"By accepting people for who they are."

"I try to keep people motivated."

"Through service to others."

"Through my acts of work or achievements. They speak for themselves."

"By doing what's right."

"Through sincerity and compassion. I believe spirituality is in every one of the virtues that are in the Bible: patience, joy, love and kindness."

"I try not to say anything cruel. I'm very critical and I'm trying not to judge people. That is a very big thing for me."

"By identifying with people who are going through tough times and giving them a word of encouragement."

"By not hurting anybody."

"Being a friend. Trying to be considerate of other people. Trying to put myself in someone's shoes and situations. Trying to be humble."

"By raising children. Being there for them and anybody else who needs my help."

"Trying to instill spirituality in my daughter so that she is not as slow about it as I was at her age."

"Being true to myself. By being honest and loyal."

"By being a mom to my son."

"Through relationships, whether it's my husband or work."

"To be very sensitive to other people's needs."

A forty-one-year-old woman from Colorado expresses her spirituality "through my family and making the home life good for them and a place people would like to be."

A thirty-year-old Chicago pediatrician expresses her spirituality by living. "I wear bright colors on the pediatric floor. I tell a joke in the middle of something horrendous to help somebody when everything breaks lose. It is a marvelous thing. By being who I am and not being afraid to support other people in their own endeavors. This includes crying with a family when everyone is crying. It's very spiritual."

"I chose to work primarily with women and students at the junior college and Head Start families through art," said a forty-eight-year-old woman from Colorado. "I have a large number of women who don't validate themselves, do not know their worth. They have knowledge within themselves that is not only useful to them, but to others."

For an executive director from Colorado, one of her loves in life is to see women who are not sure of themselves suddenly start to blossom. "Many of my staff are women who have been out of work for a period of time. They are unsure of themselves. But they blossom in their image of themselves. I see that as something very important to me."

"Through everything I do," said a forty-six-year-old astrologer. "Everybody is here to do a certain thing, a certain mission. We have to find out what it is. Once we find out what it is, that's half the battle. The other half is doing it."

Kathy from Georgia described her beautiful spiritual expressions and also presented a question for us to ponder. "I learned to express spirituality by three things I say in the morning. 'I will open myself up to receive love.' 'I will love unconditionally.' 'I will accept what is.' Can you imagine learning to accept a person for who he or she is, and not what you want the person to be?"

And Irma, a sixty-nine-year-old homemaker, expresses her spirituality when the day starts "with Jesus. I put my feet on the floor and say, 'Thank you Jesus. I can get up and walk. I'm here. I'm alive. I give You all the glory. I praise You.' "

Spiritual expression is very sacred to us women. It is our unique soul offering to God.

Self-Reflection

Think about your answers to the following questions and then take a few moments to do the exercise. Your answers and actions will help you see the connection between your daily actions and your spirituality.

Questions for Meditation:

- ✓ How do I express my spirituality?
- ✓ How do I see others expressing their spirituality?
- ✓ How does expressing my spirituality make me feel?
- ✓ How do I feel when I observe others expressing their spirituality?

Exercise: Mental Conditioning

Think of the phrases you have heard throughout the years that discourage you from reaching out and performing an act that expresses your spirituality. A few examples are "Don't talk to strangers," and "Mind your own business." Evaluate how you may have been conditioned to repress your spirituality. Now, move past those barriers. Take an extra step. Do a random act of kindness for someone in need to expand your spirituality. It could be something as simple as buying a breakfast sandwich for a homeless person or something as grand as volunteering your time with a local charity. Observe how your acts impact others and encourage you to do more.

Chapter Thirteen
Moments When a Woman Feels the Most Spiritual

"It's an euphoric feeling, a closeness to God."

Pam

W hen does a woman feel the most spiritual – the clos- est to God? Is it a special time in a woman's day? Evening? Morning? Or is it a significant moment in a woman's life when she feels that little bit of heaven on earth?

If I were to choose one question that I enjoyed listening to the women's responses the most, this would definitely be the one. I found it fascinating to hear how the women managed to juggle their times and their lives so that they would have special moments to connect with their spirituality.

The women's responses were awesome, but very realistic and easily identifiable for all of us. As one woman simply explained, "I need to be alone. I go into the bathroom and take a long leisurely bath. Or when my husband is working nights and my daughter is away at school, and I am home alone, then I have free time to communicate with God." Another woman described her spiritual moments as a special feeling in the mornings. "There is a moment when I am just awakening. I am one with myself. It's a very peaceful feeling."

We all need some special time to call our own when we can reflect on our life and our spiritual nature. Unfortunately, many women are afraid of the silence, of being alone, and of feelings of guilt. It's okay to take five minutes for ourselves. Without some alone time – even as little as five minutes a day

– women quickly get overwhelmed and burned out. With all the hats women must wear today – wife, mother, employee, caregiver, etc.– it's easy to forget to make time for ourselves, but it's a necessity we cannot ignore.

Many women claim that they're so busy that they can't spare a moment for themselves. In those instances, it's important to grab the seconds whenever they come, whether it's when you're standing in the grocery store line or listening to music. Whenever possible, take a few minutes to reflect and relax so you can feel revived both physically and spiritually.

In the women's own words, let's hear them describe the moments when they feel the most spiritual. Their moments are listed under various geographical locations, so you can see, as I did, how common and universal our spiritual threads are, wherever we may live.

From Alaska:

"When I feel love."

From Oregon:

"When I'm with my friends and bowling."

From California:

"During jazz dance."

From Colorado:

"When I'm in the mountains in Colorado, listening to Yanni music, and with my son or someone who is very special to me."

"In the wilderness."

"At night, under the moon."

"Mountain streams. In nature."

"When I look around and see people. The other day I saw a man hugging a child. It gave me this sense of peace inside."

"After I've done something to help somebody else. I've gone out of my way to do something that I didn't want to do, even if it is taking care of somebody's baby for two hours and changing diapers. I knew that person really needed that special help."

"A friend and I are working with a Spanish family. The mother is from Mexico and has seven children. We are buying shoes, coats, and things for the last month, helping them out."

"Times I am sharing in depth with another woman and really connecting on a deep level"

"When I am with my children."

"When I'm in bed with the man I love."

"It happens when I'm in the car and I have a really deep need for something and I hear a song on the radio. It's real direct encouragement and need."

"Last night after I left the play and listened to the radio. The music was so incredible."

"When I'm true to myself. When I allow time to just do what I know is important in my life."

"When I see results for either asking or it just comes about. Sometimes, it is not the answer that I was looking for, but I do know that it is the answer."

"Through my career, when I'm successful."

"My exercise time is my spiritual time, when I talk to God."

"Having this baby is going to be a real inner strength."

"When I've been through a difficulty."

"When I was ill."

"When I'm down, usually when I'm in a crisis."

"Out of prayer and meditation and knowing I have been somewhere very deep."

"With a group of people whose intent is to pray."

From Missouri:

"On the Sabbath. That's a special day, because you have church services and you are conscious of the day being a Holy Day."

From Quincy, Illinois:

"When no one else is around and it's real quiet in the house. My husband's out of town or he's sleeping. My son is sleeping and I have a cup of coffee."

"When I am praying with someone, a friend who just had surgery. It's not a proud spirituality. It's a humble spirituality."

"When I'm standing at my daughter's bed at night. She says her prayers and I kiss her. That just tears me up, because it's a miracle that we have her."

"When I see my husband and son walking in the park together."

"When I am in church. The music is playing, I am singing, and I give the kiss of peace, which is the handshake. You give your hand to people behind you who are total strangers."

"When I see my son standing in front of the church with other four and five-year-old children singing the older Christmas songs."

"When I sit in church, that touches my heart."

"At Christmas Eve when I hear *Silent Night* and the candles are flickering in the church."

From Chicago, Illinois:

"When I'm swimming or when I go to the health club or whirlpool. It is just something with the water and me. It feels so peaceful. I look up and I can see the sky. All my ideas come."

"Just sitting here, now, and seeing the delineation between the black bulky building and the mist on the lake. It has something to do with seeing purpose. That is something to be noticed, enjoyed and appreciated."

"When I'm walking in the rain, like I was today, or when I'm driving along the lakefront and I am looking at the glory of God all around me: the buildings, the water, the sky, clouds and birds. That's when I do the most talking to myself and am very spiritual."

"When I go down to the beach and I stand and watch the water. When I go to see my parents and all my relatives who live in the country. It is so different from the city."

"When I'm out walking by the trees."

"Outside. It really doesn't matter if it's raining, snowing, sleeting or sunny. To be able to be away from people."

"When I am working in my garden watching the grapevines harvest. It always reminds me of the fruit of the vines."

"In the morning, because it is quiet and peaceful."

"When I wake up in the morning and see everything around me, I have to say: 'Dear God, thank you for this day. Thank you for everything.' I wake every morning early. I don't know why we are so lucky."

"When I am by myself. There doesn't have to be a sound in the house. There doesn't have to be any noise anywhere. I could be in the kitchen cooking and it will hit me. And the water rolls and I say: 'Thank you, Jesus.' Because I know then that there is the Master reaching out to me. Whatever, it will be okay. I am crying because of happiness. Enlightenment. Joyful!"

"When I have a weekend off and am able to sleep for twenty-four hours, which is more of taking stock of what has happened and replenishing it. Those are the glasses of wine, the bubble baths, the magazines and giving myself a manicure. Just thinking, long walks and nothing else."

"When I'm alone I do a lot of talking to God. I can be honest and truthful. I am at peace and I am resting."

"When I'm alone and not around other people and distractions."

"Mostly during the day with people either at home or work."

"When I learn something new and understand it. It has to do with being connected to time. If there's no change then there's no movement in time."

"When I have deja-vu experiences. It's the feeling I have been here before or when I know what's going to happen next and it happens. That is when I feel the most spiritual."

"With a group of friends and sharing stories."

"When I am with a friend who is disabled."

"With my daughter. When she performs on stage or when she is devastated about some event. It's motherhood. The day she was born, I think was one of the most. That inner feeling of being connected with my child."

"When I am at my absolute lowest and there is no where to go, and my back is up against the wall, then I pull it out. I can lean on my spirit."

"When someone is ill in my family."

"When my sister died."

"During a crisis."

"When I truly go to worship. I mean, I am not just in church for ten minutes, but when I'm truly there to worship."

"I don't have one particular time. I have been extremely touched in prayer or reading a scripture passage that I might have read five million times. I got nothing out of it before and then it hits me. Those layers are pulled away and I see it a different way."

"On high holidays, like Yom Kippur, the Day of Atonement, when I have to fast for twenty-four hours."

"Sunday, when I go to church. I feel like I'm recharging my battery and it gives me that charge to get through the week."

From the northern, southern and western suburbs of Chicago:

"Being outside in my yard, looking in my pond and watching my fish swim around."

"Being able to enjoy a beautiful nature day. A sense of calmness and not being worried about everyday things."

"Camping."

"When I'm alone in my bedroom by myself."

"When I sing."

"Music."

"When I'm feeling strong and I am in a position where I made the right decisions and others respect me. I feel good about it."

"When I wake up in the morning and when I go to bed at night."

"When I'm driving my deceased husband's car. His car was his baby. I get in the car in the morning. I rub my hands around that steering wheel and know maybe somewhere on that steering wheel his fingerprints are still there."

"When I look at my family and I walk through the door."

"When I'm rocking my baby at night."

"Saying and talking to other people about things that are important. Sharing things."

"With a spiritual dear friend."

"Being with that particular person and knowing that he could be the most important person in the world."

"There are times when there are deaths with my patients."

"When I am with somebody who has a great deal of distress and really needs somebody to talk to. I sit and listen or give them a hug."

"When my baby almost died."

"I have to be honest when things aren't quite right. The spirit is always there. Deep down inner feeling really come out when I hurt. When I feel like I really need somebody: a mother, a father or a best friend. God is always there. He's there."

"When I am most touched emotionally."

"When my spirits are low. I have to have somewhere to go."

"When I go to bed at night, that's my time that I get into prayer and I thank God for whatever has happened through the day, for what I think and I feel. Strength when I'm at my weakest point."

"Right now, after my husband had a quadruple bypass. I realized how close and lucky I've been. I do not forget through prayer to thank Him every day."

"When I'm closest to the Lord, when I am in church by myself and more reflective."

From Indiana:

"When I'm talking with someone about the Lord."

"When there is a tough situation coming up, I feel spirituality more. I can feel myself depending on it."

"When I am grounded, together, and flow with life."

"Reading the Holy Bible."

From Wisconsin:

"In the morning when I wake up and I am being renewed for another day, and at night when I go to bed and I am being safe with God. May your Light be my sun this winter day."

From Alabama:

"When I'm by myself saying my prayers."

From Georgia:

"I live out in the country. When I drive through the countryside and see all the products made, I think of all the facts I found out about God. Being a Christian just amplifies it."

"When I'm out in nature, because this world is so beautiful. I'll tell you something I heard a movie actress say: 'If you feel you are getting a little too big for your boots, go out and look at the ocean.' "

"When I'm sitting beside the ocean and in the mountains. Being with my fiancé's little boy. He is five years old. Sometimes when we are together, he says things and puts his arms around me. It's incredible. It is really spiritual."

"In the morning when I wake up."

"In my car by myself with the radio off."

"It happens all different times. A lot when I meditate. When I'm in the car listening to music. I open myself. It's almost a euphoric feeling. I get it from time to time. No pattern."

"When I am giving or helping someone to help themselves. Not necessarily just helping someone out, but to definitely know that I am guiding them in that direction."

"It doesn't have any rhyme or reason to it when it hits me. It just comes upon me and I can't figure out what it is that makes it touch me. That is what makes me feel like it is something much more powerful than anyone can see."

From Massachusetts:

"When I am focused by myself. Private times on my own, as when I'm in my car and the radio is off, because I don't want to be distracted."

From Washington, D.C.:

"When I slow down. In the mountains or if I am in the middle of the city and slow down, I can feel it."

There was a twenty-five-year-old woman from Indiana who saw and felt heaven on earth. Here's her story. "My sister's fiancé and I were heading out to Washington, D.C. in his old beat-up recreational vehicle. We were heading for Virginia to pick up my sister. We said a prayer before we set out traveling. We decided to take his recreational vehicle on the Blue Ridge Mountains since I had never seen mountains in my life. We took Skyline Drive. When we started at the base of the mountains, I said: 'What is that smell?' But no one listened to me. It ended up being the brake fluid. We descended down the mountains and it never occurred to me that we were on a mountain overlooking other mountains. We were on a very steep hill and he did a pull over. I saw so many stars in the sky. I never saw so many stars in my life! It was one of the most beautiful times that I ever felt so close to God! I knew a great peace then. I knew He was going to be with us and we would get off the mountain safely. It was so beautiful!"

Lessons From Our Sisters

If there's one thing we should learn from these responses it's that we women desperately need to steal a few moments each day so we can marvel at the wonder of the world. Whether we find some solace in nature, in friends and family, or in some act of creation, it's those moments that can revive our spirits and touch our souls.

When we feel the most spiritual – when we have that deep innate feeling that goes to the depths of our souls – that is when God is reaching us, keeping us focused, and giving us His guidance and love. It is our little bit of heaven on earth.

Self-Reflection

Think about your answers to the following questions and then take a few moments to do the exercise. Your answers and actions will help you see how you use alone time to revive your spirituality.

Questions for Meditation:

- ✓ When do I feel the most spiritual?
- ✓ What is it about that place, event, or time that connects with my spirituality?
- ✓ How can I make more time for myself on a daily basis?

Exercise: Stealing Moments

How can you make time for yourself and your own spiritual reflection? Think of the many times during the day when you are alone – perhaps it's when you're having a cup of coffee in the morning or when you're sitting in your backyard listening to the birds sing. During those moments, rather than listen to the radio or dwell on your challenges, revel in the silence and in the images around you. Use that time to really look at the world and all the positive things in your life. Try it today. The feelings you experience will amaze you.

Chapter Fourteen
A Woman's Difficulty with Spirituality

"Just living day by day in this world of ours, where priorities are so different than the Lord."

Mary Beth

Is spirituality difficult for women? Only fourteen of the one hundred women stated that spirituality had "not been difficult" for them.

"It is just part of me."

"It has been a growing process through every cycle in my life."

"I don't think any of it has been difficult."

However, eighty-six out of the one hundred women clearly stated that spirituality was difficult for them. Quite a few of the women explained that their particular difficulty with spirituality was "trying to fit spirituality into the mainstream of life, because it is not a spiritual society." It was "the contradiction and confusion that we are all faced with today."

While the idea of spirituality itself is not difficult, many times we make it difficult in our day-to-day lives. We let our mind's barriers towards spirituality keep us from experiencing it. However, the more we push our spirituality away, the more difficult and challenging our lives can become. Concepts such as "life purpose" and "happiness" seem elusive. In my own experience, looking back I now realize that if I had not put my spirituality on the back burner after I turned 14, my growing up years would have been a lot easier. I would have had someone to connect with and turn to during trying times. Even today, as I face life's challenges, I need to constantly remind myself that spirituality is not difficult.

A thirty-year-old design trainer for a software company echoed the same message. "Living by what I believe has definitely been the most difficult. I can walk out of my church and feel like I'm on cloud nine. The emotions are there. The whole world seems beautiful, and then just ten minutes later out of church, I get in a traffic jam or someone will cut me off and I lose that feeling. So hanging onto that and living by it is the most difficult."

A thirty-nine-year-old Chicago woman spoke within the same context. "I tell myself I'm going to make a change, like I'm not going to gossip anymore or I'm going to love everybody or I'm going to be patient with people. Then I go to church on Sunday and I commit to it. Monday morning comes. I have the Monday of all Mondays. The six-week staffing schedule is due to be posted. I have a staff nurse telling me that she can't work this schedule, and so on. All of that [what I did on Sunday] goes out of the window. It makes it very difficult to be very loving, forgiving, patient, and understanding."

"Sometimes when I'm doing something, I know that what I am doing does not agree with my spirit. My flesh wants to do something while my spirit wants to do something else. Nine out of ten times my flesh wins and I end up repenting," said a thirty-four-year-old woman.

A thirty-year-old investment wholesaler from Georgia vocalized how difficult it was "trusting the universe to take care of me when I am in a cash flow crunch or when I am sick."

A couple of women simply said that they had "very busy" lives and were just "crowding spirituality out."

Several women explained that their particular spiritual difficulty was accepting and understanding spirituality, "the concept of the intangible." As one woman said, "Blind faith – that has been hard for me to accept."

A twenty-seven-year-old computer specialist and word processor strongly questioned and wondered at times: "Why is something happening to me in my life? Why is nothing going right?"

A forty-one-year-old teacher, mother and wife vocalized that, "Sometimes in my low points, I feel that God is not fair."

"There was a time that I couldn't grasp it, that God didn't understand me," explained a sixty-six-year-old mother and grandmother.

"I can only try to answer to myself and hope for the difference between understanding and acceptance," explained a forty-five-year-old Chicago woman. "I can understand something and not accept it, but it is more difficult to learn to accept things without understanding. That's a tough number."

A few of the women informed me that their main spiritual difficulty was with patience – that wonderful, but very trying, virtue. So often in our lives, our souls are face to face with this very important virtue.

As a forty-five-year-old Chicago woman explained, "Learning to be patient and to wait. To believe in something I can't put my hands on and can't feel."

"Coming to grips with the time it takes for the results. I know it is going to happen. But sometimes I experience things and I want to see results. Then I ask, 'How long? How long?' It just takes time. It is that old hand that says, 'He may not come when you want Him, but He is on time.' It is at that time that I am the most contented with what I am doing," said a forty-three-year-old woman from the Midwest.

A few of the women stated that their particular spiritual difficulty was with the whole issue of control. For example, a thirty-one-year-old woman from Georgia said: "The hardest part has been letting go. I'm a control person. I have to be in control."

From the snow-capped mountains of Colorado, a forty-nine-year-old woman described how this difficulty impacted her life through a skiing accident. "When I don't have any control, I don't know the depth. About six years ago I fell through ice during a skiing accident. I injured my back and had surgery. I was in constant pain. In that situation I had no control."

Quite a few of the one hundred women stated that their spiritual difficulty was "being around a lot of people who are not spiritual." As one woman explained, "Sometimes it's like going into a brick wall."

For a thirty-nine-year-old executive secretary, this spiritual difficulty was with her family. "They don't understand spirituality at all."

And a woman from the northwest suburbs of Chicago explained how she had "to turn spirituality on and off before I get home."

For a twenty-eight-year-old registered nurse, this difficulty caused spiritual confusion for her. "I hear other people's view but don't always get clear directions."

"People look at me and see me living my life. People ask, 'How can you be so happy, because you are not praying all the time and won't go to prayer meetings? You don't do this and you won't do that.' I found that to be very difficult," emotionally said a sixty-seven-year-old woman.

Several women were hard on themselves, and that in itself made spirituality difficult for them. "When I don't feel spiritual enough. It's like a constant search. It is frustrating when I don't get answers or a sign," said a forty-year-old police officer.

For a thirty-one-year-old Georgia woman, "The difficult part comes with the fact that I don't believe I have reached my inner peace."

"I'd like it to be easier," said a fifty-seven-year-old Colorado woman and "not to fight with faith all the time."

One woman simply said, "I try to bargain with Him and I should just have more faith."

A fifty-one-year-old woman from Colorado had to release the thought of "not feeling condemned because of God. The hardest thing was to work through, in terms of tapes, in terms of myself, and negative talks."

One woman humbly said, "Believing in the fact that I did things wrong. Forgiveness is divine."

A few of the women had particular difficulty with living by certain doctrines of their church. A fifty-five-year-old security officer, mother, and grandmother emotionally told her story to me: "It was difficult when I was divorced thirty years ago. I was very young and angry at the church because they wouldn't baptize my son. I felt they let me down."

"I was married before. I had difficulty with the relationship and the precepts of the church," sadly explained a fifty-five-year-old Chicago woman.

A forty-one-year-old director of childcare institutions strongly believed that "spirituality is difficult when people confuse it with religion."

Nancy from Chicago believes a woman's spiritual difficulty is with the fact that "women are inclined to think we can fix things. We have some of the roles as nurturer, caregiver, guide, instructor and controller. We feel something enough that we want to share it. We want other people to feel it too. We want to be at peace."

When I questioned a psychologist from Alaska about her difficulty with spirituality, she responded with a philosophical question for us to ponder: "From what point of view? From the ego not to be crushed?"

Thirty-two-year-old Kathy from Colorado presented a societal perspective to a woman's spiritual difficulties. "I don't think society encourages women to be spiritual. Because I accepted a career, which is an owner of a day care center and a consultant, that is very acceptable for women to be in, I don't have many conflicts. I have a friend who is an attorney. Her husband is an attorney. She is not the motherly type. She works hard and is looked down on, but he is not. If I try to venture out in the male corporate world, I'm sure there would be more obstacles."

Carol described her spiritual difficulty and passed on some very powerful soul advice for us to ponder. "It is easy for my life to become so complicated that I don't take the time to access those things that I know would keep me completely together. At times, I have to access the internal core of my spirituality. I am now making decisions about what I want to do, because high-powered traditional jobs do not allow time to do those things. To me it's the whole question of the pace that is expected, because of the cost of your soul."

So what can we do to alleviate the difficulties?

Whatever our spiritual difficulties might be for us as women, they are our personal soul challenges that we will face in our lives. By having a better understanding about the spiritual struggles of other women, we will be able to help each other, because we are never ever really alone.

   There are wonderful supportive human beings all around us – our friends, families, working buddies, and our neighbors. They are there for us. We need not be afraid and look the other way, but instead slowly glance toward them. They can be a light for us. Maybe, it was your neighbor, who, on a particular day when you were emotionally down, casually said to you, "Hang in there. Everything will be better by tomorrow." Or perhaps a dear friend empathized with you by saying, "I understand what you are going through; I've been there." Or someone at work kindly said to you, "Let's go and have a cup of coffee and talk about it." Sound familiar? God sends these very special people to us, and maybe even angels, to help us in our lives.

Self-Reflection

Think about your answers to the following questions and then take a few moments to do the exercise. Your answers and actions will help you see how determine how easy or difficult spirituality is for you.

Questions for Meditation:

✓ What do I find difficult about spirituality, if anything? Why?
✓ What do I find easy about spirituality, if anything? Why?
✓ What can I do to alleviate any difficulties?
✓ How can I help others who are experiencing similar difficulties?

Exercise: Understanding Difficulty

Write down a particular difficulty you have with spirituality. Think about your answer and how and when the difficulty transpires. Is it during a family interaction? When you're alone? When you're stressed? What makes it so difficult during those times? What can you do to turn that difficulty into strength? When you know specifically what the difficulty is as well as how and when it transpires, you can take action to overcome it.

Chapter Fifteen

How Spirituality Eases a Woman's Life

"Spirituality gives me an inner peace that is unexplainable."
Mari Lee

"Spirituality is the soft pillow every night. It's the blue skies in the morning!"
"It made my life great."
"I wouldn't have been able to get through another day without it."
"It's like a burden has been lifted off my shoulders, and spirituality made life easier."

These are some of the responses I received when I asked the one hundred women how spirituality had eased their lives.

Ninety-eight out of the one hundred women clearly told me that spirituality had definitely eased their lives. And surprisingly, only two women out of the hundred vocalized that they were "unsure." Only two! That is how powerful spirituality is in a woman's life.

Spirituality is, in essence, hope for women. When we draw on our spirituality during challenging times, we display our strength to "give the problem" to God so we can get through the event. We acknowledge that by ourselves we may not be emotionally strong enough to handle the situation, so we turn to a Higher Power for comfort and insight. It's then that we have the inner confidence and self-assuredness to go through life and meet our challenges head on.

Let me share some of their responses with you.

"When I was praying for my son to come home from the Middle East War, and he did come home safe, I was beside myself. When one prays for something so hard and then one gets it. Wow! " exclaimed fifty-year-old Rosetta.

Twenty-six-year-old Anita emotionally told me how spirituality helped her with her mother's death. "Mom died at fifty when I was twenty-two, maybe twenty-three years old. I knew I could never have gotten through life and the certain pains and things in life if there wasn't a God."

"It is hard to raise two kids by myself," explained forty-three-year-old Rose. "With spirituality on my side, I feel like I always have a hand in whatever I am doing. Whether I have a good day or indifferent, spirituality is always going to turn me onto that right pathway."

"Having a relationship with God has made a big difference, because I feel His strength. I can receive from heaven through my relationship with Him. I have seen God do things in the lives of family members. That makes me more aware that He is there and He's not going to abandon me," said a thirty-seven-year-old marketing coordinator, mother, and wife from Atlanta, Georgia.

Sarah, a forty-year-old police officer echoed the same. "Knowing that love is always there for me. All I have to do is ask for the Lord. He will always see me through the most difficult things. He will be there for me. He will never give me anything I can't handle. He will never do that. He is omnipotent."

Liz from Georgia told me that she is "learning to let go and let God. I just turn it over to Him. It makes life a lot easier."

Quite a few of the women explained to me how spirituality had eased their lives, in personal intimate ways, such as helping them to have:

"Peace of mind."
"A sense of hope and acceptance."
"Calmness."
"Security."

"Faith, confidence, and strength."

"A release. A comfort."

"A balance. An inner strength."

"An outlook. A sense of humor."

"Doubts alleviated."

"Answers."

"Hatred taken out of one's heart."

"Faith that things get better."

"Acceptance of things and people for the way that they are."

"Control over one's life. Not to worry about things."

"Ability to deal with stress."

"Ability to get through some of the tough times."

"Hard times easier. Not have fear."

A forty-six-year-old Chicago woman explained to me how spirituality has helped her progress from the point of wanting things in life to the point of acceptance and gratitude for what she already has. "My husband doesn't make much money and he probably never will. We are never going to be rich. My kids will never be geniuses. They are not going to be famous musicians. You come to a level of acceptance on a lot of things. Much of it is wanting. I figure that I have a bed, a refrigerator with more food than I can possibly eat, and clothes on my back. Thirty thousand babies die every day of starvation in this world. What am I complaining about?"

As Leah from Chicago echoed, "The quality of life is more important than the quantity of life."

From Colorado, a forty-four-year-old woman, explained that spirituality has caused her "not to be so uptight as I used to be. It's letting go. That is what spirituality is. That is a purpose. When I'm at my best I am thrilled to be alive. That's what it's done. A connectedness. It's like I can look out at a sea of people and smile. I know that we are part of each other. It's like we are evolving. Spirituality is not stagnant. I don't know what's ahead of me. I don't know where it's going to lead me.

I don't know what plan we are going to be brought into. But I want it."

Barbara, from beautiful Georgia, passed on a soul provoking response for all of us to strive for, "Spirituality is the most important thing in one's life. If we are gifted enough to see that, and borrow that path, then we will be led to true enlightenment."

That is where we are all headed or we would not have picked up this book to read.

Self-Reflection

Think about your answers to the following questions and then take a few moments to do the exercise. Your answers and actions will help you see how spirituality eases your life.

Questions for Meditation:

- ✓ How does my spirituality ease my life's challenges?
- ✓ How do I feel my spirituality during trying times?
- ✓ What do I do or say when I turn to my spirituality?

Exercise: Embrace the Light

Write down your answer to the following question: "How does spirituality ease my life?" Notice the feeling that washes over you, and stay with it. Feel the warmth of peace and the love of God. Let it become part of you. That feeling itself – that inner peace or serenity – is what helps you ease your life. So answer the question and whatever you feel, stay with that feeling and encompass it in your being.

Chapter Sixteen
Barriers to a Woman's Spirituality

"There will always be more doors to open, but it's just knocking down one door at a time. For every peak there is a valley."

Denise

Have you ever felt something about spirituality or a certain life experience that you just could not understand, grasp, or even accept? Maybe it was something deep inside of you and very difficult for you to release from your soul. Was it that "something" that caused you to close the door to your soul and delay your spirituality to a later time in your life? Or did you just close the door to your soul altogether? What was that barrier that had such a profound impact on your spirituality?

More important than the barrier itself is what a woman does when she is face to face with that specific spiritual barrier. How does she open the door to that very special part of her soul and allow the beautiful warm light in?

Ninety out of the one hundred women interviewed stated that they had definitely experienced a significant barrier in their lives that had a profound impact on their spirituality. The women's barriers are listed below under a general theme heading. Next to each is a compilation of the special advice from the women as they addressed their particular barrier. Now, let us slowly open those doors to our spiritual barriers.

The Barriers

Lack of Understanding

- Trying to figure what it was all about.
- Wondering if there is a God.
- Trying to understand God's perspective.
- Lack of knowledge about Jesus Christ.
- Ignorance. Not knowing about God.
- The statement that God said: "Heaven and earth will pass away, but my word would never pass away." I couldn't understand that.

Advice

Keep searching for your answers. Continue to pray. Realize that God's will shall be done. As long as you are faithful, available, and teachable, He will bless you, because He said He would. Read the Bible, and sincerely believe every living thing has spirituality. See it in a tiny plant. Everyone and everything is a thread in the fabric. Get the answers you need by asking others. Don't be afraid to ask.

My Own Thinking

- Being too intellectual about things.
- A need to know everything.

Advice

Keep it simple. You may need to leave your intellect so you can have spiritual experiences. Have faith in those helping you. Have experiences that are true for you.

Religious Aspects

- Negativism towards structured religion.
- Changing religions.
- Confusing religion with spirituality.

Advice

Move beyond negativity by going to the church that makes you feel good. Do what your heart is telling you. Meditate to find out who you are. Believe in yourself. Do not automatically accept the precepts of another person, religion, or group. Test it out for yourself and find out what your boundaries are and acknowledge them.

Spiritual Choices

- Choosing spirituality.
- Choice of wanting to be spiritual or denial.
- Initial experiences with spirituality.
- Spirituality is hard work.
- I have to admit spirituality is a process. At times, I have doubts and that is the biggest obstacle.

Advice

Ask yourself, "What is the barrier? What are your reasons not to choose it? If you choose it, what do you believe about it?" Spiritual things are not fake. Don't test God. Give Him the opportunity to help you. You will always have challenges ahead of you. Nothing will happen overnight. Hang on. Find good friends. You'll get there no matter all the emotions you'll go through. Don't live without spirituality. That would be death. Life can be very exciting. It's faith. It's not rational. You can't control it.

Daily Challenges

- Day to day hassles wear on my spirituality.
- Getting enough faith to do it.
- Not having the support. My soul is hungry for more.

Advice

Join a meditation group and meet regularly. Don't be afraid of your spirituality. Trust your spirit. Trust God. It works! Your spirituality is always there. You have got it! You don't even have to look for it or seek it. It's there for you. Just let go. Experiment within yourself. Think about yourself and the best person that you can be to the world. Start acting on that and see how your spirituality comes back to you. You are making your contribution from your heart. When you start getting all the rewards that come back, you know that has to be.

Issues of Control

- I'm a strong person and I have to yield to God.
- Questioning why other people weren't spiritual.
- Listening to other people.
- People tried to shut me down.
- Learning to live together.
- Need to control the situation.
- Letting go of control.
- Stubbornness.

Advice

Take off all your trappings, everything that is you, and then stand before the Lord. You are just yourself, none of the trappings, not the cute clothes, just you. You are there with Him and baring your complete soul with Him and can just cry your heart out. Others are the way they are be-

cause they haven't been able to reach that point and really believe. Sit down and look at what is going on. Look back when you were a child and what you fantasized about. Who did you really want to be and how have you gone astray. Try to get back. Realize that you need spirituality in your life to become a whole person. Without it you are not complete. You need to have faith in others before you can have faith in anything else. Once you develop that faith, and you work and live together, you then exchange ideas by the way you live. Accept the concept that a superwoman is a farce. Instead, develop your spiritual growth. If you fail in something, realize you are not a failure. Trust yourself, your feelings, and others. Don't be afraid to have intimacy with another person. Above all else, accept. That is the biggest advice. That is the biggest challenge.

Fear

- Fear of change.
- Out on a limb.

Advice

Keep digging. Become the friend of God. Wait through the period and realize that things happen in life the way they are meant to happen.

Negative Mindset

- Judging life through a materialistic viewpoint.
- Cynicism.
- Too many things stand in the way.
- I believe in anthropology and archaeology – that was my major. Biggest problem over ten years was how I could make these two things work together for me.
- Living in a communist system.

Advice

Become spiritual. There is an end to it. You need to find something meaningful, even if it is selfish. Look for the little things – the little miracles. Sit and think about the event and impact on your spirituality. Believe and celebrate with your friends and family.

Illness and Disease

- Wanting to lose weight.
- Alcoholism.
- Anger with having breast cancer.

Advice

It has to be something you want to do. Don't do it because someone is telling you. If your heart tells you to do it and it is going to make you feel good about yourself, do it for yourself. Don't do it to please anyone else. Care about your-self. The way out of any situation is to want help. Ask for help and allow other people to help you.

Death

- Losing my mother at a young age and then my father becoming ill.
- My mom dying.

Advice

God will give you no more than you can carry. Pray for inner strength. Time will heal all wounds.

Family Issues

- My mother accepting the church's position against birth control. She had five children.
- My father, being a strong born-again Christian.
- Having strict parents.
- My parents had a very unhappy relationship.
- My family, my home life, when I was young.
- Growing up in a chaotic family.

Advice

Look at the comfort faith gives people. Let go. The world is open to you. Open yourself to everything. Look at yourself. Discover what makes you happy and what level you want to go to. That's something you have to find for yourself. Be comfortable with it. You are going to survive. Care enough for yourself to be happy. We are meant to go through a certain path. Sometimes we go astray and sometimes we go off on the wrong turn. It was meant to happen for you, because you will make a difference in someone's life knowing what you know. Read your Bible. Get to know what the scriptures say. Any problem you will have will be in the Bible, if you just look for it. Tell your family that you are sorry they are not in the same place as you. Feel good about where you are and where you are going.

Teenage Difficulties

- Being a teenager and caught up in living.
- Peer pressure. Being busy and losing sight of spirituality. Didn't take the time out.
- In high school I didn't ask for guidance from above and then later, I didn't want to go to church.

Advice

Take time for spirituality. These are the years you really need it, because you go through so many changes. You don't have to do it alone. Sit down and talk to someone. Search out a group.

Life Phases

- A phase when I was twenty-one and didn't believe in anything.
- Various phases of my life when I felt I wasn't coping too well with things.
- Living a wild single life and not thinking about the consequences.
- Lack of guidance and direction to identify things.
- Distraction. My lifestyle.

Advice

Do not fight it. It doesn't do any good. Spirituality comes from within. It's not up in your brain. Feel it and work your way back. You will feel the time. You need to connect with friends and need to let them into your life. Take some time off, even if it is locking yourself in your apartment for a weekend or going for long walks. Think about what you are doing and where you want to be twenty years from now. Stop! Slow down. Look at your life. Be strong and do it. You will be much happier. Truly want to figure it out. We don't all have the same right of passage for spirituality. It helps to have some solid people who are sounding boards and who can help you reflect on who you are and what you are doing. Find people who can give some real insight to yourself. These people can give you answers. They can also ask you the questions that help you start looking at yourself. Keep focusing. Don't lose it. Spend time by your-self.

Marriage

- When I got married and unwound from my single life.
- My husband and I had different religions.
- Loving a man not from my faith.
- Staying married to my first husband.
- When I was divorced and had no faith for many years.

Advice

If you are in touch with somebody, you can truly enjoy that person. Listen to what each other is saying and listen if it makes sense. Believe what you are doing. Keep your life going. Above all else, look out for yourself because nobody else will. You have to start thinking about you, only you. Be honest. Be true. Be loving to people who are truly your friends.

Personal Discipline

- Being lazy and not disciplined with my spirituality.
- Not having any time for spirituality.
- Just my own discipline with spirituality.
- Learning to be patient, to wait, to believe in some thing you can't put your hands on.
- Understanding.

Advice

Go back to discipline. Make the time. Meditation is essential. Everybody has the same twenty-four hours; nobody has more time. Question what life is all about. Pray, because your spirituality is connected with someone else – God. Communicate with Him. He will tell you what you need to know and He will show you. Listen to that inner voice

*that never fails you. Just sit back. Be quiet and wait. Find
a place that you know is your place and is peaceful, such
as in a church, your room, a lake, or whatever. Go to it as
much as you can, even if it's at the expense of doing what
you are supposed to do.*

Personal Guilt

- Overcoming guilt and opening up.
- I didn't feel I was good enough in my organized religion.
- Self-confidence.
- Being shy when I was young.
- Every time something went wrong, I wondered why.

Advice

*Be gentle with yourself. Add that extra whipping cream. It's
not going to add up. It will come up. If you don't like your
current church, leave. God is everywhere. Like yourself.
See your inner beauty. Your spirituality will get you through.
Get strength. A lot of people will guide you.   Listen and
talk to God. He'll direct you. He'll give you that inner
strength to go on.*

Depression

- Being very unhappy and preoccupied.
- Being able to come to terms with what I want in life. Being honest about my values and being willing to confront myself with them upfront.
- Giving my life over to the Lord.
- Giving up.
- Working through God's inner tyranny and being happy with me.

Advice

Unravel where all that unhappiness is coming from. Then look at yourself and get that unhappiness out of you. Think spirituality. Pull yourself up with it. Come to terms with yourself, and that's hard to do. Once you find spirituality, once you realize you have it, don't let go. Keep developing and nurturing it. Listen to others who might help you understand more about what the Lord wants. Don't push yourself, because the Lord will walk you through. It is worth it, even if it doesn't seem like it is at the time. You don't actually give up. You gain. Believe that God loves you unconditionally.

Self-Acceptance

- Learning to accept myself.
- To recognize who I am. What are my drives, motivations, and needs?
- Being comfortable with myself.
- Respect myself.
- Myself.

Advice

Accept yourself in whatever avenue you need to accept yourself in order to love. Once you achieve that, then look back. There will always be more doors to open. Keep knocking down one door at a time. For every peak there is valley. Value what you are sure of inside. Don't worry about anyone else until you take care of yourself first. Then love yourself first, before you can love others. Be honest with yourself. Make a very structured contract with yourself. What starts off as construct can become natural. But don't do it alone. You need a support group. You need to have someone to share your experiences with who can help you and bring them nearer to you. The experiences are there, but you can't see the message. You need time. Go with the flow. Listen to your gut. Do what you think is right. Also, surrender to God. Acknowledge Him. Desire this. He will bring this about. Sometimes growing in spirituality can be painful.

Open the door and let that warm beautiful white light into your soul!

Self-Reflection

Think about your answers to the following questions and then take a few moments to do the exercise. Your answers and actions will help you overcome your own barriers to spirituality.

Questions for Meditation:
✓　Which of the described barriers do I identify with?
✓　Does the advice make sense to me?
　　Why or why not?
✓　How can I incorporate some of the advice
　　into my life?

Exercise: Removing Barriers

Visualize yourself in front of a closed door. You can't open that door because it's a barrier to your spirituality. Ask yourself what is preventing you from opening the door and moving forward on your spiritual journey. Listen to your answer, for that is the special key. You now know the barrier, so take yourself out of the picture and visualize that it's your daughter or friend who is facing that barrier, What advice would you give them to open that door? Stop, listen to the advice you give to them, say it out loud, and then follow your own advice. What a freeing moment for you!

Chapter Seventeen
The Impact of a Woman's Spirituality on Others

"Spirituality is something I feel in my heart, and I share it with others." **Christine**

Does a woman's spirituality have an impact on others? Does it extend beyond the self and inspire, encourage, and touch the souls of other human beings, such as children, family, friends, or co-workers?

"Oh, yes!" exclaimed Leah. "I see it in the people I have touched and the people I spent time with."

Peggy joyfully echoed the same by saying, "Yes, because it is so much a part of life, with my friends, relatives, and family. Spirituality makes me the person that I am."

Eighty-seven out of the one hundred women interviewed definitely agreed that their spirituality had an impact on other people in their lives, not always a profound impact, but a quiet impact that permeates the soul.

The Root of Kindness

In many ways, the impact of spirituality was a reflection of the kindness women display every day. And often, it's those little acts of kindness that go a long way towards helping others and enabling them to feel special.

"It [spirituality] has a big impact on my true friends," said Nancy from Indiana. "The relationships have grown deeper and more loving. They are people I know I can count on through life for anything. It is a friendship of spirit."

Jenae from Washington, D.C. said, "With three girlfriends. There was a connection between all of us. We were all on a search. That part was awakened and we were being attentive to it."

Thirty-six-year-old Alice explained how her spirituality helped her seek friends who are spiritually oriented. "It's like a deeper, quicker relationship."

Donna from Georgia sadly recounted how she supports a friend who was treated unfairly by a company she was working for. "I help a friend of mine who became unemployed. They fired her when she was on maternity leave. She has two small children, a three-year-old and a nine-week-old. I tell her she will get through this."

"Definitely, my sister," proudly said Liz from Georgia. "I've seen her turn one hundred and eighty degrees since we started living together two years ago. I have seen her go from not having any spiritual path to having one. She was like a little flower bud. I've seen her bloom."

A sixty-five-year old grandmother proudly told me, "My grandchildren prayed at my dinner table. I told them to bow their heads and pray, and they all prayed. I was surprised. And, one night my daughter, who I am trying to get back to church, said to my little granddaughter: 'Marie, you pray now.' And she started to pray. She prays so nicely. When I pray or talk or say things to my granddaughter, she knows. She tells me: 'My grandmother is going to heaven, because she goes to church all the time.' I am surprised that she listens to me."

Bobbie, a fifty-seven-year-old mother, lovingly spoke about her college-aged children. "My children are away at college and I'm not down there with them. But my son and daughter are there together. They never miss Mass. My daughter tells me that her brother always goes to confession a couple times a year."

Forty-eight-year-old Jackie said with motherly pride, "My daughter. She is so God-like. She is such a sweet and understanding person. I thank God that, with His help, I paved the way for her. I am so proud of her. She is now twenty-one years old."

"When our daughter was sick she would call me up with her problems and say to me: 'I feel I can come to you. You always try to put me in the right direction and you don't judge me. You say what you are feeling. You don't tell me what to do'," lovingly told forty-four-year-old Lana.

Forty-four-year-old Sue said, "It is neat to watch my daughter. She will be seventeen years old. She just got back from a church conference, which has made the biggest impact on her – twenty-eight thousand teenagers all in one place."

"My two children are evolving, so the jury is still out," cautiously said a forty-five-year-old mother. "But they have a sense of sharing, giving, and loving."

Impact on Men

Many women explained that their spirituality impacted the special men in their lives.

"My husband has a different philosophy," lovingly explained a forty-one-year-old woman from Quincy. "He is Catholic like me, but his belief in God is that he doesn't have to go to church to be with Him. He believes God is there when he is running or biking. The moment our child was born he felt God was there because this was a creation that only God could create."

"My husband. We just fit everything, even physically. We just fit so well. We both felt we were soul mates. Everything!" warmly said a thirty-eight-year-old customer service manager, mother, and wife.

"My inner strength has helped my husband. He is a strong person from the outside, but inside he needs a strong person to help him through the hard times. I have helped him," explained forty-nine-year-old Kathy.

Forty-eight-year-old Charlene told a powerful story about her father. "One day my father read St. John and then just quit drinking. He read John twenty-three, which said: 'I am the way to the truth and the life.' From that day on, in 1972, he never drank again."

Unlikely Impacts

What's amazing about spirituality is how it can rub off on the most unsuspecting people. Fifty-two-year-old Annetta surprisingly said, "My spirituality has rubbed off on my first babysitter. She always tells me I was the strength in her life."

A forty-nine-year-old child of God, nutrition consultant, mother, and wife, as she delightfully described herself, said, "In my job, I have touched people who don't let the Lord be first in their life. I feel like I have helped people put that to the forefront of their day."

"In terms of a colleague of mine, she thought of me when she converted to Catholicism," warmly told a twenty-nine-year-old Chicago woman.

"I see the impact of spirituality when people need me," said thirty-six-year-old Terry. "People are uncomfortable talking about spirituality because it is different. It is not in sync with the world as we know it. People will see one side of me. They never in years will believe some of the things I like to do, such as go to church or say the rosary. They look at me and question: 'Really?'"

"In all relationships," pointedly said a thirty-four-year-old woman. "When I was young I was more temperamental. Spirituality has calmed me down, like a pleasant and peaceful control."

"By the change in me and how I have gotten through the rough times" said Joan, a secretary from Chicago. "My best friend has complemented me many times. She is so proud of me."

Void of Impact

Three women believed that their spirituality did not have an impact on others. "No, I don't think so, because I'm not that outward on how I feel," said one woman.

Ten women questioningly said, "I truly don't know if I made a difference in somebody else's life."

Many times in our lives our spirituality will transcend and reach out to others, whether we are aware of its impact or not.

It may be a noticeable impact or a silent one. Regardless, it comes from the depths of our souls. It is a warm bright light that is connected to God. It is shining to inspire, encourage, and touch others.

Self-Reflection

Think about your answers to the following questions and then take a few moments to do the exercise. Your answers and actions will help you see how your spirituality impacts others.

Questions for Meditation:

- ✓ How does my spirituality impact others?
- ✓ How do I know of the impact?
- ✓ How do I want to impact others?
- ✓ How do others impact me?

Exercise: Conscious Kindness

For one day be very conscious of your actions. If it's helpful, write down all the small things you do for people during the day. Record people's reactions to your kindness as well. Too often we lose sight of what we do and whom we impact. But when you're conscious of your actions and deeds, you can apply them so you're leaving an impression you'll be proud of.

Chapter Eighteen

With Whom Does a Woman Discuss Spirituality?

W hen a woman wishes to talk about spirituality, about those things that touch the depth of her soul, to whom does she turn? Who do we ask to join us for dinner or for a cup of cappuccino after work to discuss our daily struggles, dreams, and aspirations? What number do we automatically dial on the phone when we need to talk about the personal things that touch our souls? A personal friend? Our sister? Our mother? Who are we most comfortable with?

When I asked the one hundred women if they were able to discuss spirituality with their friends, seventy-five of the women stated that they freely discuss spirituality with their personal friends, because there is a level of comfort that exists and is understood amongst them. Plus, we get to pick our friends, whereas with family we don't have that luxury. So we tend to befriend people who are like-minded and who are on similar paths as our own.

"More with my friends than my family," explained twenty-three-year-old Jenae. "In a lot of ways it's a connection with my friends. I have a desire to see them grow on their journey, and I know they have the same desire for me."

"I have two friends whom I am very fond of and I easily talk with them about spirituality," warmly said sixty-six-year-old Stephanie. "They enjoy hearing and listening about spirituality."

Thirty-nine-year-old Patricia from Wisconsin said that she discusses spirituality in a casual and spontaneous manner with her friends. "It could be on the phone, in the car, in a house, in a restaurant, or on the street walking and talking about what a beautiful day it is. It just comes up!"

Twenty-nine-year-old Donna from Stone Mountain delightfully described her spiritual conversations with her friends. "We usually do get into it with one another. You have to have a good spirit and a good soul if you want to attract good people with good spirits and souls. Whatever you are, that's what you will attract."

"I discuss it with most of my friends, but I do try to be careful," cautiously said one woman. "I don't want to force on people something that they think might not be important to them. If they are not comfortable with it, I don't force it."

Thirty-year-old Liz from Georgia explained that she discusses spirituality with the men she dates. "It used to be that my spiritual friends were primarily women, but now they are men, including my boyfriend. In fact, that is the one thing my boyfriend really respects about me – my spirituality."

Fifteen women stated that their discussions about spirituality are dependant "on the friend" and the "closeness of the friend" because, "there are different levels of friendship."

Ten women stated they "never" discuss spirituality with their friends. As one woman explained to me, "I have two women that I have been friends with since I was six years old. We have never discussed our spirituality with one another. With one of my friends I don't even know what church she goes to." A sixty-year-old woman added, "I never discuss politics or religion."

The Family Tree

When I asked the one hundred women if they were able to discuss spirituality with their family, sixty-eight of the women stated that they freely discuss spirituality with their family.

"Oh, yes. We are a healthy group of faith who argue a lot," said a thirty-year-old woman who was raised in a devout Jewish and Catholic household.

"I do with my children. It has made an impact on my sons and daughter. On Christmas Eve the whole family gathers for a Polish dinner. We break the wafer and have a seven-course meal. We are not supposed to leave the table during the Christmas Eve meal, because that is the one time we are all together. It symbolizes that the family will be together forever. Grandma brought this tradition all the way from Poland and it has been our family tradition for three generations," lovingly said Stephanie.

"With my sister I discuss it very freely. With my parents it's getting easier, because they came from a different generation. They have a very structured way of practicing their spirituality, and it's not the same as mine. We don't expose ourselves to the same thing. We both say prayers and know there is a God, but we took a different path," explained a thirty-year-old Georgian woman.

"Very free," said a forty-eight-year-old woman from a rural setting in Colorado. "My mother has spent all of her life trying to figure out what her spirituality was. I saw that going on through my entire childhood, and that search for a religious base was always very open and accepting. There is never any rejection. I am not required to hold a particular view. That is very accepting."

Thirty-six-year-old Terry lovingly told me that she had discussed spirituality with her parents when they were alive. "My mother would tell me that God comes first. For all the things God does for you, the least thing you can do is give Him an hour of your time." Terry warmly told me that her father started to talk about spirituality with her when he became older. "He really evolved and started to go to daily Mass. Before he died of cancer, he would tell me that now is the time for him to have faith."

A proud mother told me this little story about her daughter. "I have a seven year old who is so receptive. Have you ever seen special children? She is more alert than a seven year old.

She isn't intimidated by me. She walks on faith. She is a very strong soul."

Twenty-seven women stated that they definitely did not discuss spirituality with their families. As one woman pointedly said, "I wouldn't feel comfortable talking to them about my beliefs."

A thirty-nine-year-old woman echoed the same. "I do not discuss spirituality with my family, but I do with my friends. I don't think my family is on the same level. My mother has never spoken to me about spirituality. She is a very private person with her feelings and thoughts. My whole family is the same."

A twenty-six-year-old secretary told me that she could not discuss spirituality with her family, "because they are all angry."

And thirty-one-year-old Lisa from Denver, Colorado sadly said, "Not at all, because they think I'm weird."

Five women stated it "depended" on the family member. As a thirty-year-old woman further explained, "With certain members of my family, such as my brother, my mother, and my sister, I can. Not with my Dad, because he tends to lecture. I can't start the discussion. I have to keep it superficial."

A fifty-year-old Chicago woman echoed the same. "It depends. With my son I can discuss it freely. With my parents, barely."

"I can probably talk to my daughters, but not my sons," said a fifty-one-year-old woman.

"Some of them I can. I don't know if they are old-fashioned or if their way of thinking is one way. Some of them probably thought I was crazy talking to them about it," said a forty-one-year-old Indiana woman.

As forty-year-old Sarah wisely explained to me, "I feel like I should discuss it, but for some reason it doesn't come up in the conversations. I think people view it as a taboo subject. To some people it is a very intimate subject. To me, it is part of living."

So, let's live!

Self-Reflection

Think about your answers to the following questions and then take a few moments to do the exercise. Your answers and actions will help you identify why you connect spiritually with certain people.

Questions for Meditation:

- ✓ With whom do I discuss spirituality? Why?
- ✓ Do I connect more with my family or my friends? Why?
- ✓ What makes me open up to one person and not another?

Exercise: Expand a Friendship

On a piece of paper, make a list of people you feel comfortable discussing spirituality with. Why do you feel such a connection with these people? On a separate piece of paper, write down those people you feel you cannot discuss spirituality with. Why do you think you can't talk to these people about the topic? What could you do to bridge the gap and open up to these people? Maybe you could invite the person out for coffee and bring the topic up in conversation. Who knows...it could open up a whole new aspect of the relationship you never knew existed.

Chapter Nineteen
The Importance of Spirituality In a Male-Female Relationship

"It is important to see that other human being as part of God."
Victoria

For the women who are married or are in long term relationships, what keeps you together with your man, in the good times and the bad? Could it be that there is a very special spiritual bond that exists just between the two of you?

Do you remember the chemistry, magnetism, or energy that attracted you to each other when you first met? Did you experience that special knowing in your souls that you were destined for one another?

Could it be that when a woman falls deeply in love with a man, she is truly falling in love with his soul, that very special part that is connected to God?

Ninety-six out of the one hundred women interviewed clearly stated that spirituality was very important in a relationship with a man. Did you hear that positive response rate? Ninety-six out of one hundred women. Now, that's a statement!

"Spirituality is a wonderful thing to have in a relationship," said a forty-one-year-old executive director from Denver, Colorado. "It is love that leads to our understanding of each other."

"It is seeing God in one rather than our projection from a limited mind," explained a forty-three-year old psychologist from Alaska.

Violet wisely told me that "spirituality is the bonding that comes between people. It's tied in with one's understanding of what life is all about and building for the future. If two people are in a relationship, they should have some kind of understanding of each other's spirituality. It is what makes us tick!"

"I honestly believe that to really love at the deepest level, I need to share my spirituality," explained forty-three-year-old Karen. "The man should be the spiritual leader, says the Holy Bible. I want someone to teach me. I don't want to be the head."

A sixty-five-year-old woman from Chicago explained to me that in her culture the "Native American Indian women have no competition with our men. We work side by side. It's one of those things that I learned at an early age – respect."

"My husband and I are very different, because he is a very spiritual person," vocalized a thirty-one-year-old Colorado woman. "How we go about it is different. We both have an element of it. It is like a ladder and everybody is on a different rung and we are just trying to keep going."

A thirty-year-old woman from Georgia concurred and explained further that "men and women are different. Not only do we live differently, we think differently. Therefore, you have to have a spiritual base if you are going to make a commitment in a male-female relationship. If you have that spiritual base, then the option for a solid strong commitment is there and you have a point of reference to go back to."

"I remember reading a Lynn Andrew book," said Julianne, "in which she said that marriages don't last because couples don't have the intellectual, sexual, spiritual, and emotional combined. Usually one of those directions is missing. Couples can be relating on the intellectual, emotional, and sexual level, but if not on the spiritual level, there is no balance."

Forty-three-year-old Hope pointed out: "When everything else fails, spirituality is the one thing that holds us together. It is how things are connected. That is why marriage is an important step."

From Georgia, a thirty-seven-year-old woman sadly explained the importance of spirituality in a relationship, "because I've seen what could happen when it's not there."

"Spirituality is very important in a relationship," said a thirty-seven-year-old registered nurse, "that's why I'm still single."

"Relationships are a lot of trouble and hard work," said a forty-five-year-old Chicago woman. "If both have a belief beyond themselves, there is a tendency to be less hedonistic. This is more of a willingness to compromise, empathize, and sympathize and to feel." And as she eloquently added, "I will compliment his weakness and draw from his strength."

An Issue of Trust

Surprisingly, only one woman out of the one hundred interviewed replied with a resounding "no." As one woman said, "There are many parts I don't share with my husband, and spirituality is one of those parts. We have been married twenty-five-years and I'm used to it."

Three women did not respond with a definite yes or no. Instead they said such things as: "I'm not sure. It would be nice." "I didn't quite think about it that way." And as the third woman said, "You have to have certain things in common. I don't know if I would say the word spirituality."

For this question, I purposely focused only on the male-female relationship. However, spirituality is important, as Martha said, "in every relationship." For this is how we touch, understand, and love each other. If spirituality is missing in our relationships, we may find a lack of depth in how we relate to each other, and we may discover that superficial actions may be all that holds us together.

The ninety-six affirmative responses from the one hundred women interviewed was a profound statement on how important women feel that spirituality is in a relationship with a man. "How could it not be?" pointedly asked a fifty-five-year-old Chicago woman. "How could someone be that committed to a person in a relationship without spirituality?"

Sounds logical, doesn't it? When it comes to male-female spirituality connections, trusting each other with our inner-most self is important. But if you are not comfortable sharing your spirituality with a man, don't worry. People change, and God's hand is in everything. We are here to help each other along the journey.

Comfortable Communication

Since spirituality is that important in a male-female relationship, do men and women really discuss it with each other? Are men comfortable discussing the topic of spirituality with women? Are women comfortable discussing spirituality with men?

Sixty-eight women out of the one hundred women interviewed stated that they found men to be very comfortable, as they were, with discussing the topic of spirituality.

"Surprisingly, in the last relationship, as devastating as it seemed to be, one of the big things and the key part of the relationship was that search for spirituality. That was one of the biggest attraction we had for each other," said a thirty-eight-year-old woman from Indiana.

A forty-one-year-old woman from Illinois echoed the same. "Yes, I've always been easy to talk to. I met this man whom my ex-sister-in-law tried to fix me up with. On the day we met we were having a drink in a restaurant, and we started talking about reincarnation and how we all come back at different levels."

"Yes, and now since I have been divorced, I feel more and more comfortable with discussing spirituality with my ex-husband and the present man in my life," explained a thirty-four-year-old Chicago woman. "I will never push that subject away again, because something would be missing in my life. I feel the men who are comfortable with talking about spirituality are comfortable with themselves."

"Yes, there always was that conversation when I dated someone," said thirty-six-year-old Terry. "It seems that conversation always comes around the fifth date, the conversation that ends all conversations. Then everything pours forward and spirituality always comes up. Men seem to be angry about it, because I think men like to be in control. It is part of a woman that a man can't just get at."

"When men and women talk about spirituality, they are both on the same place and have compatible spiritual values. If you have the same spirituality, that to me is as important as having intimacy and communication. Communication can be a spiritual communication that one person, that one soul, gives to the other soul," wisely explained thirty-seven-year-old Christine.

From Birmingham, Alabama a forty-seven-year-old registered nurse, mother, and wife told me, "I come from the South, and Southerners are very vocal about their religious background. We are in the Bible belt, so you have to take that into account. When I lived up North, no. It depends upon your religion."

"I am ninety-one years old and men speak more openly than they probably would if I was your age," vocalized Mary.

From Illinois, a fifty-two-year-old woman regretfully told me, "My husband and I talked about it somewhat. He died four months ago. I wished we would have spoken about it more."

"Yes, but not many [men do] and they are in the minority," explained a thirty-nine-year-old executive to an U.S. firm. "I think men hold back because we live in a society that thinks it is not the macho thing to do. Men are more in touch with different aspects. They are more in touch with the intellectual, the competitiveness. They are not in touch with the spiritual side, because the other parts of them are so developed. Because of that I think it is hard for them to step back. Then there are men who have no problem with it. I think men would really like to get more in touch with it!"

Forty-year-old Angela concurred. "Some men are comfortable and some are not. I think men are afraid to talk about it. It takes a lot of strength to say, 'God, I can't do this without your help.' Most men can't. They might have those feelings raging within themselves, but men in our society have been taught to not express those feelings."

A wise twenty-three-year-old woman from Washington, D.C. relayed to me that "men are so hungry for so many things that their subculture won't allow. It is not acceptable within the male culture to express spirituality. Men stay close to so many people, and when they find one person they trust, which usually is a partner, the floodgates open, and you are the only person to whom they confide. It's not a fair situation."

"I haven't felt they were uncomfortable," explained a thirty-nine-year-old Chicago woman. "I feel that men as a whole are more reserved about everything. I don't know what they talk about with their own group and their male bonding. But my husband talks to me about his beliefs, and he relies on my beliefs to get him through. He says, 'You have a halo around you and I want in on your halo!'"

Thirty-two women out of the one hundred women interviewed stated that men were not comfortable, as a few of them were, with conversing on the topic of spirituality.

"I think men deal in tangibles. They deal in things that they can actually feel. I'm generalizing and I realize that. But look at my dad. He's an engineer. My boyfriend is an engineer. I think men, especially in the science background, want to prove it. However, it's too intangible to imagine God rising. I just think it's too far-fetched for a lot of men because they figure their intuition must be shut down," explained a thirty-year-old software design trainer.

"I think it is more uncomfortable for males to speak about spirituality, because I think they have been brought up thinking they should have all the answers. A lot of men have been brought up thinking that they don't need to look to someone else for the answer. They do not want to become vulnerable, and you have to become vulnerable in order for someone else to give you the answer," warmly vocalized a forty-seven-year-old director.

"It's a subject that men tend to shy away from," said a thirty-four-year-old Chicago woman. "They leave religion, spirituality, and things like that up to women."

"I don't know if it is a thing with not appearing macho or what, especially with the black heritage," explained a forty-three-year-old woman. "They have a thing about letting their guard down. I think if they would really think about it, it wouldn't be quite as painful as they seem to believe. But for some reason they can't open up."

"For the most part, I think men are uncomfortable because they are inexperienced. I think they are not aware of what might fill them up and don't know that it is already there and waiting to be revealed. Women have been aware of their spirituality on a traditional basis. I think it is perfectly acceptable that some men fall off the track rather than women being on the track. Women have always had to be many, many things, depending upon what room they were standing in and what day the week it was. Men don't have that advantage. It does allow us to be comfortable with this piece. I wish that I were a sociologist or anthropologist. Men were hunters and women were gatherers. Think about what is involved physically in hunting versus gathering. Which one allows introspective thinking? Which one allows nurturing? What's inside can come up and out. It's that simple. That is why women are the way they are, and men are the way they are," stated a forty-five-year-old woman.

"Ninety-eight percent of the men I meet have two interests on their minds, business and pleasure. Society has done it to man. They feel it is effeminate and not masculine to pursue passive activity. They have been taught to be tough. They are taught that to develop the spiritual is not masculine. Isn't that a crying shame?" questioned a forty-one-year-old woman from Atlanta, Georgia.

"It's because of me. I'm not comfortable with talking to men about spirituality. It's not them, it's me," said a thirty-eight-year-old Colorado woman.

"Men don't bring up the subject very much with me," said a thirty-one-year old woman from Georgia. "I had trouble with relationships, because spirituality is my core. I can't find the man who is open enough to have this type of discussion with me."

And as one woman simply told me, "It's the part of me that I don't share with a lot of people."

Approximately one-third of the women I had interviewed were not able to communicate their most intimate thoughts on the topic of spirituality to their significant man. How is it that we can ask someone to share our lives with us as our companions and yet not be able to discuss our soul thoughts with each other?

"We are all like a puzzle," profoundly stated Cynthia, "Without spirituality there is a part of you that's missing." Could this be the missing piece of the puzzle for woman and man?

Self-Reflection

Think about your answers to the following questions and then take a few moments to do the exercise. Your answers and actions will help you identify how spirituality impacts your male-female relationships.

Questions for Meditation:

- ✓ With which men do I discuss spirituality? Why?
- ✓ Am I comfortable talking to men about spirituality?
- ✓ Do I talk about spirituality with men the same way I do with women?
- ✓ How can I make it easier for men to discuss this topic with me?

Exercise: Be a Man!

Look at the various men in your life: father, husband, brothers, friends, etc. After you identify which ones you can discuss spirituality with and which you can't, list the reasons why there's a difference. What specifically do you say to those you can talk about it with compared to those you can't? Is it something in your language style, choice of words, body language? How do those men talk to you? Is it different from how females talk to you? List what you can do to "speak" the man's language. Then, try what you've uncovered with a few men in your life and notice the reaction and the difference. Modify your approach based on your feedback.

Chapter Twenty
The Emotional Spiritual Connection

"Emotions are a part of the highs and lows in God's presence."
Rita

Have you ever experienced a special moment in your life, attended a spiritual ceremony, or visited a very special location that touched your soul and had a tremendous impact on your emotions? Perhaps it brought you to tears and onto your knees in adoration of God.

Maybe it was the birth of your child, whom you had carried in your body, heart, and soul for nine months. Perhaps it was when you survived a fatal car accident, because your guardian angel had turned the steering wheel that brought you to safety. For some women it's attending midnight Mass in the beauty of a candlelit church. For others, it's skiing on a freshly powdered mountain twelve thousand feet up in the heavens with no one but you and God's magnificent universe. Just recently for me, it was on the sacred ground of the Church of the Annunciation in Nazareth in the Holy Land where the angel Gabriel appeared to the Blessed Virgin Mary and she said, "Yes."

Could there be a connection between a woman's emotions and her spirituality? Ninety-two women out of the one hundred women interviewed clearly stated to me that their emotions were definitely connected to their spirituality. Only two out of the one hundred women believed there "was no connection."

An emotional connection to spirituality certainly makes sense, because when you experience a profound event, you feel an internal response that is so much more than the event itself. As ninety-one-year-old Mary from Chicago told me, "Oh, yes. I'll be sitting over there listening to television. Suddenly a song comes on or the actors say something and tears will come down on my cheeks when I'm not even thinking about crying. It just affects me in that particular way, that particular song, that particular incident. It just touches my soul."

"When I am in church and the preacher is preaching and singing, it's like all the emotions build and it's almost one," said fifty-year-old Rosetta. "I can't have one without the other."

"The day I was married and the time my son was born, I knew God was there. It was a happy emotion and I thanked Him," said forty-one-year-old Victoria. "Another time was the day my father passed away. I knew that God took him in a peaceful caring way and that my dad was happy. God was taking care of him and I thanked God. So for my part, emotions are involved in my spirituality."

As a twenty-six-year-old Chicago woman told me, "People definitely express their spirituality through emotions. Just like when I was sitting in your office the other day, I got something from you and I started crying. It was some kind of spirit of feeling that was beyond me."

"Spirituality is closely connected to the emotion of love. You need the love aspect, because love is so important to spirituality. If you have love, you will be able to forgive," said thirty-nine-year-old Kate from Chicago.

Francille, who described her age somewhere between forty and death, believed, "When you are emotionally struggling, you come to spirituality. When people are on their deathbed they become believers. I heard friends speaking during the last war about what life and God meant to them, because they felt united through that."

"That's a really good question," said thirty-year-old Jean, "because the more mature someone is in his or her spirituality, the more mature he or she is emotionally. You stop taking things so much at face value and are able to progress to a higher level."

A few of the women told me that "spirituality gives tremendous control to emotions," as stated by a fifty-year-old advertiser.

"I can control myself more, because I know it's not going to do any good to let off steam and let everything go out of proportion," pointedly said a sixty-six-year-old housewife, mother, and grandmother.

Thirty-eight-year-old Mary echoed the same. "Spirituality keeps the balance without tipping the scales. My spirituality won't let me tip the scales to the point where I am off the deep end. It keeps the balance."

"If you have strong faith, it will help temper the emotions in a crisis situation. It takes the feeling of hopelessness away," said Marilyn a forty-six-year-old registered nurse.

Violet, a sixty-seven-year-old retired nurse, also emphasized that "spirituality helps to keep the emotions under control. It is the bigger influence on the other."

A thirty-year-old investment wholesaler from Atlanta, Georgia said, "Emotions are a choice we make. We choose how to express them in each life given situation. We have to choose how we are going to react to it. Spirituality can cause you to feel a whole different emotion."

"To me, spirituality reflects people's emotions and the way they feel. Spirituality gives inner peace. It reflects in behavior. There is a certain type of glow that is attached to a spiritual person. I think it is more of a vibe," reverently said thirty-seven-year-old Christine.

Twenty-five-year-old Mary Beth from Indiana believes that "a spiritual person tends to be a more happy person. The Lord gives peace and allows for a happier living."

"When you are nourishing your soul, you have a positive attitude and outlook on life. You respond spontaneously and positively," warmly said a forty-eight-year-old Native American Indian woman.

A fifty-year-old widow explained to me that "spirituality guides me to what I need. When you are very emotional, such as expressing happiness, sadness or grief, you tend to be more focused in your spirituality."

"Some people think spirituality is all emotions, or all in your head, heart, or a fantasy. I think it is whole. People in Denver get emotional about football games. So I really don't know why I shouldn't get emotional about my faith and my relationship with God to a certain extent," explained fifty-seven-year-old Eugenia from Denver, Colorado.

Forty-three-year-old Karen from Quincy, Illinois passed on an insightful analysis on the subject of the emotional and spiritual connection. "People can confuse emotions and spirituality. A very emotional person isn't necessarily a spiritual person. If someone is very spiritual, the emotions go right on the surface. It's not an expression. It's their spirit. Emotions and spirituality are very close. Sometimes, you hear of people on an emotional high, but that doesn't mean spiritual. However, a spiritual high is an emotional one. It's always the heart, not the head."

Six out of the one hundred women interviewed believed that emotions and spirituality had some connection. As one woman explained, "It depends. I don't necessarily think all the time. One has to think about spirituality. Sometimes, I will be very angry and explode out the worst things and spirituality has nothing to do with it. First, I have to get rid of the emotions and then my spirituality can evolve. Emotions are feelings that everybody has. If you are talking about a spiritual relationship with God, then you have to rid the anger. Otherwise there are obstacles."

Another woman said, "Emotions and spirituality can have some connection. Emotions, like feelings, are transient. There is such a change from day-to-day. But spirituality is there; it stays."

So perhaps we have always been talking about spirituality, but calling it a different name – emotion. Since spirituality and emotions are so connected, it only makes sense that women – the ones labeled "emotional," "sensitive," and "feelings-oriented" throughout history – would be more in-tune with it. What are your special moments, spiritual ceremonies and sacred grounds that bring tears to your eyes and adoration of the Divine? Believe it or not, you already know the answer, because you have been there so many, many times in your life.

Self-Reflection

Think about your answers to the following questions and then take a few moments to do the exercise. Your answers and actions will help you discover your own spiritual-emotional connection.

Questions for Meditation:

- ✓ Which events have elicited a strong emotional response in my life?
- ✓ How did those events impact my spirituality?
- ✓ Are my friends and family as "emotional" as I am?
- ✓ How can I help them through an emotional time?

Exercise: Examine Your Emotions

Recall the last time you had a really hard cry. What was going on inside you? What were you pulling from inside? Also recall the last time you laughed so hard that tears streamed down your face. What was that feeling? Relive it now. As you do, realize that our joys and our frustrations are gifts from God. These emotions help us get our soul to the next level. What do you learn about yourself and your capabilities at these moments?

Chapter Twenty-One
The Women Who Embody Spirituality

"Their life is a continuous thread around their beliefs and value systems that is unending."

Carol

Have you ever known a woman who seemed to embody spirituality? When you are with her, you personally experience a spiritual high. It is as if your souls touch each other for that moment in time.

Who are these special women who make heaven on earth for us? Can words even describe what we feel and see when we are around them?

Remarkably, ninety-six of the one hundred women stated that they definitely had known or seen women in their lifetimes who embodied spirituality. Even better, they were able to describe what they had felt, seen, and experienced when they were around these women.

Who Are These Women?

"Women in the creative arts," stated Nancy from Indiana. "It is accepting one's God given talents. Those are such wonderful talents. It is a joyful way to show spirituality. It is a recognition of soul."

Patricia from Wisconsin said that she feels and sees spirituality in women dancers. "In their dance they show an exuberance in how they engage in life and enjoy it."

For forty-three-year-old Rose, spirituality was embodied in her grandmother. "She was a great woman. My grandmother would say things that I knew were coming from another place. She saw my path, and through her prayers and God's guidance, it happened for me."

"My husband's grandmother is one of those sweet persons who exudes spirituality. How do you describe it?" pondered Jennifer. "It's like a sweet gentleness that you feel. She is comfortable with herself. I tend to look for this in older people. They are wiser and experienced down the road."

Rita warmly said, "My mom. She had a strong sense of faith. Her advice was, 'You could miss life by just walking through it. You have to stop and take a look.'"

"My mother," said twenty-nine-year-old Mary Jane. "She had good values. I hope to pass those values on to my daughter. She had strength. My mother never had anything bad to say about anyone."

Zenaida sentimentally reflected and joyfully said, "My mom! She was very spiritual and a service to others. She was the counselor for a little town in the Philippines. She would take care of sick people. If a woman was in labor, she would stay with her. She was also a teacher, and that's what I probably saw in her. I never realized she was spiritual till now. I thank you for that."

"My mother-in-law. She would take complete strangers from the streets into her home if they needed a place to stay. Our house was like a restaurant for anyone on the streets. If my mother-in-law wasn't cleaning or cooking, she was in the church. She was someone special. When she died at age fifty-six, she was thoroughly loved. She was the type of person who never expected anything. Everyone remembered her. When little kids in the neighborhood grew up and became men in their twenties, they knew they could stay there with my mother-in-law and have a place," lovingly reminisced sixty-year-old Marge.

For twenty-seven-year-old Sally, spirituality was embodied in her great aunt. "The woman is a joy. I never heard a bad thing come out of her mouth. She's always doing something for someone. She is always nice. She always makes me feel comfortable, and spirituality oozes from her. It just amazes me that somebody could be caring and considerate all the time."

"My sister is one," proudly said thirty-eight-year-old Mary. "She has a quiet unspoken spirituality and love. She has almost a classiness and a sophistication that comes from her. She is someone I admire."

A Friend Indeed

Quite a few of the women witnessed spirituality in their personal friends or through simple acquaintances. It's amazing how spirituality easily fits into our complicated lives. Now, let's read on to hear about our special friends and acquaintances.

"In my friends, I see inner goodness flowing outward. I have a good feeling when I am around them. Positive stuff. It's not negative. I can actually see a glow flowing outward. I can feel it," beautifully described forty-eight-year-old Jackie.

"Friends of my mom," explained twenty-six-year-old Anita. They had an aura about them. They knew what they wanted and nothing could stop them. They knew where they were and were totally focused. Those are women that you rarely find, but you can spot them."

Seventy-four-year-old Marion also described spirituality as it is manifested in her friends. "They reach out with affection. They express it through hugs or words of grace to another person. They are comfortable with any situation at any time. They don't fall apart. They stand up for truth and what's right. They call the shots the way they see them, and that comes from character. It is all part of it."

"A lady friend of mine who is sixty years old," said Francille from Missouri. "She is the sweetest person. I see it in her all the time. Her kindness and thoughtfulness. I just love to be with her."

"The lady that just walked out of my door," exclaimed a forty-year-old woman from Quincy, Illinois. "It's something she exudes. It just oozes out of her. She is a neat, neat lady. She is one with herself. She is at peace with herself and with her family. She has a very close relationship with God. She shows it in the way she acts. I see it in the things she says, in everything about her."

Forty-three-year-old Karen observed spirituality in acquaintances. "I see it in the way they talk, their voice and their eyes. Everything. It's unbelievable."

A sixty-three-year-old advisement coordinator for the Institute of Native American Indian Development witnessed spirituality in her friends by "the way they live. The way they talk. They raised their families by themselves because some of them are single parents who have lost their husbands or are divorced. They have something that is so radiant, so happy."

"Friends and acquaintances. Gentle people. Confident people. I am attracted to their positive energy. They make me feel at peace and make me feel warm and protected," said thirty-seven-year-old Christine.

"Friends," joyfully explained Charlene. "They are so bubbly. They have a gregarious attitude."

"Friends, family, and acquaintances," stated a thirty-year-old-pediatrician. "I have seen people and thought to myself, I want to have this person over for a dinner party. There is something about them. It's a comfort with themselves. Sharing. They share so easily with themselves and others, regardless of intelligence, education, finances, or whatever. I've been impressed with clerks on the patient care ward, as well as housekeeping. It's a sense of decency and giving to people."

"In my friends I see charisma. That's a difficult question," said fifty-six-year-old Ruth from Indiana. "I want to say an aura, but I don't. It's a vibrancy."

"My best friend. There is a peacefulness. An acceptance. There is a non-struggle. There is a giving, along with being human," warmly explained forty-seven-year-old Ellen from Denver, Colorado.

For fifty-seven-year old Eugenia from Denver, Colorado spirituality was seen in her friend who was a nursing supervisor. "She had severe back surgery, and then her husband died of skin cancer. Her life has not been easy. Her role was really to empathize with somebody who was in pain. A gentleness.

She never got upset with people. She had a real positive attitude about everything."

"A couple of friends. There is that quality that they are not from this world. They function in between. They walk on the carpet lightly. Their feet are different. I feel a certain okayness when I am with them and the feel different when I am away from them. I feel centered. It's hard to describe," perceptively said thirty-one-year-old Lisa from Colorado.

Forty-one-year-old Kerry from Colorado described her spiritual friend who lives in San Diego. "She is very calm and patient, very loving. Her appearance shows it. She's always well groomed. I think your spirituality shows in grooming. It shows that you care about yourself and you believe in yourself, as a child of God. It radiates from people like that. A kindness, goodness and acceptance of other people."

"Friends and family," exclaimed forty-nine-year-old Genelle from Denver. "They are radiant. Loving. Their spirit. I can tell by their countenance. They bubble."

Fifty-one-year-old Jan observed spiritual embodiment in her women friends "who are able to reach out beyond themselves. They are grounded in themselves and with unconditional love for other women."

Workplace Wonders

A few of the women I interviewed explained to me that they witness spirituality in women who manifest their souls openly in the work place.

"A manager I work with," exclaimed Zander. "When I walked into my office one morning she was there. There was something about her. A glow. I picked up on her spirit. She has a gorgeous spirit."

"Quite a few in the nursing profession. They are more interested in the bigger picture of helping people. It is in their eyes and the faces. It is a serene confidence. Their body language lacks tension," explained thirty-nine-year-old Julianne.

"One of the women I work with is a stock broker," stated thirty-one-year-old Barbara form Atlanta, Georgia. "She is the president of the company. She is the most spiritual person I have ever met. She took three years of her life off, delved in, and invested in finding her spirituality. She was fortunate to do it. She is a person who oozes inner peace."

For forty-seven-year-old Nancy from Birmingham, Alabama it was her nursing director. "She is one fine woman. She shows it in everything she does in all aspects. I remember making this comment to her thirteen years ago, 'Christ is all over your face.' It shocked her and she almost took a double take. It's all over her and it's a good way to be."

"People I have met in the massage parlor. I look at them and I can feel it. I'm not sure it's physical. It is a feeling," described thirty-six-year-old Alice.

"Certain co-workers," said a thirty-nine-year-old staff assistant for childcare education. "They don't have the frowns or wrinkled foreheads. They appear content even though they have their ups and downs like anyone else does. They handle their crises in a different manner."

Religious Women

Twenty-nine-year-old Donna from Stone Mountain, Georgia described the women in her church. "They are considerate and sincere. They live this way every day of the week. These women are exactly as I see them whether it's Sunday or Friday night."

"Lay people in the Third Order Secular Franciscan from St. Peter's Church in downtown Chicago," explained ninety-one-year-old Mary. "I might say, they are of the world, but not of the world. Their actions. Their way of doing things."

"An eighty-year-old woman in my church. Every word that comes out of her mouth is spiritual. She is always a source of encouragement. She knows the scriptures like the back of her hand. She is a great teacher," admiringly said twenty-five-year-old Mary Beth from Indiana.

"The pastor's wife," exclaimed fifty-two-year-old Mary from Indiana. "She's the same all the time. Even when she is feeling bad, she is still the same. You know you can depend on her."

For forty-six-year-old Marilyn spirituality was embodied in "the nuns from the Daughters of Charity. They were not cloistered. They lived in the community where they worked."

"An acquaintance I met last summer. She was a minister. She oozed what she believed in. It was the way she expressed what she believed. A real demonstrative being," warmly said forty-one-year old Kathleen from Georgia.

"My spiritual teacher. She's attune with everything," said thirty-five-year-old Pamela. "She has a calmness about her. She's almost serene in her daily actions. Whenever I'm struggling with something, I call her for some insight. She has the answers for me."

"Two nun friends whose personalities were opposite and yet that element was there. They were very orientated to kindness and gentleness. Very good people. Something honest. No pretense about them. Very humble," explained forty-four-year-old Molly from Colorado.

"It was wonderful when I was in the convent," said a forty-four-year-old woman from Colorado. "I was with women who were on their journey and searching. They were very willing to talk about it and share their experiences and struggles. It was an absolute. It was such a fertile ground for growth for spirituality. It was a sisterhood. It was wonderful."

From Ordinary to Extraordinary

Several of the women explained that they had observed spiritual embodiment in ordinary people that they share life with on a day-to-day basis.

"Certain women are very loving, very caring," explained forty-year-old Sarah. "There is an aura around them, and I am drawn to them. It's hard to explain, but it is people that I want to be around. I want to go to them because they are very accepting and very understanding. They are very compassionate and not afraid to talk about spirituality. That is important to me. Women need it. People need it. These women are not afraid to bring up the subject of spirituality. They are not afraid. They bring it up daily in conversation, because it is a part of their lives. You sense it and then you want to talk about spirituality."

"I could name you five right now," exclaimed forty-year-old Angela. "Their empathy. Their ability to touch base with me. Their centeredness. I think that is what I most admire about them. They can have a storm raging around them, but they are centered. I would love to have it."

"There are a lot of them. They are just ordinary people like we are. There are a lot of good, down-to-earth people in my church who have gone through a lot. They are good with other people and their children. It shows all over them. I can see it in them," warmly said sixty-six-year-old Stephanie.

"People in painful situations or circumstances. I watch their reaction and their rationale. It was painful, but they are believers. They have a soft heart and a special degree of kindness about them. I've always wanted to be like some of those women. It's just like honey pouring out of their mouths. They are so sweet," admiringly said forty-six-year-old Toney from Atlanta, Georgia.

"You can look at somebody's face," pointedly said Liz, an investment wholesaler from Georgia. "You can see it in their eyes. They radiate an aura of spirituality. Friendliness. I can walk into a room and see who those people are. I can just see it."

Sandra from Illinois observed spiritual embodiment in "women who don't permit their life's crises to get them emotionally distraught. They can weather the storms of life."

For forty-six-year-old Mary, it was mostly with women "known as psychologists. It comes out in their books. They study people or hear everything. They know. They feel it. They seem to really be in touch. A lot of people in the caring professions...doctors. They didn't get there for nothing."

"I get that sense with women who are the earth-mother types – women who seem content with everything and don't question much," said forty-six-year-old Karen.

"Women who have an air of confidence, calmness, and a comfort," explained forty-four-year-old Sue. "They have an ability to give that feeling to other people. I can see the deep calmness. They don't get rattled about things. They have the countenance that they will make it through whatever is bothering them. They know it is okay to call on people to help them through. They aren't afraid to talk to somebody, because they might reveal some kind of secret or something. They are connected."

"There are a lot of outstanding women," exclaimed Julianne. "They are very strong. They have control and a real strong sense of self. They usually have a purpose in their life, whether it be their family or not, but their purpose is right. They have made their choices and have confidence that was the right choice."

"Friends and family. They are people persons. They do well in social situations and are good public speakers. They are good motivators of people and at the same time allow freedom. They are not people who direct you and tell you how to do things. They are people who tell you what the outcome should be and what one should be looking for. They let you go ahead and do it. People who are willing to learn new things and be open to new ideas," wisely explained forty-six-year-old Susan.

In the Public Eye

A few of the women identified public figures they had seen in person, on television, or in a photograph who embody spirituality to them.

For twenty-three-year-old Jenae it is "a lead singer in a rock band in Washington D.C. She is so full of life. I love being around her and other powerful women. She doesn't mince words. She speaks to injustice and straight at it. I like to see a woman who has a lot of love and goes for it. Powerful!"

"Mrs. George H. Bush. She is a wonderful lady," explained sixty-nine-year-old Irma. "She is motherly and patient. I had seen a snapshot of her, and she had her hand around the neck of the President while they were walking together. She was giving President Bush peace. It was so beautiful!"

"The perfect example is Mother Teresa. She goes through doing everything calmly, no matter where she goes. If there is turmoil, everyone gets calm when she is around," admiringly stated fifty-seven-year-old Bobbie.

"My hero is Mother Teresa," said Jo from Denver Colorado. "She is a whole person. I never met her. I don't need to meet her. I see her on television. It's there. She is the human being who has no false-self. She is living her truth self-directed by God. Her mission is life-giving. She gives herself to the poor and oppressed in the world. She gives selflessly of her entire being. She believes that God will provide in every moment. She believes that with her being and her soul."

And for Elaine, a forty-three-year-old psychologist in Anchorage Alaska, it was also Mother Teresa. "I saw and met her in India. I remember a very tiny, physical person. The most amazing thing was that when she walked into the room, grown men broke into sobs. Her words were like bullets. Her message was: 'What is healing? It is love!'"

The Woman in Each of Us

Spirituality is all around us; we only need to open our eyes and look for it. Each time we women see and witness spirituality in another human being, that same special spiritual thread is touched in each and every one of our souls. When we see, feel, and experience someone's soul, we are truly seeing God in them. What a glorious magnificent experience!

Self-Reflection

Think about your answers to the following questions and then take a few moments to do the exercise. Your answers and actions will help you identify those women who embody spirituality to you.

Questions for Meditation:

- ✓ Are there certain women I am naturally drawn to? Who are they?
- ✓ What is it about these women that make me feel "different?"

✓ How do these women impact my life?
✓ Do I view these women as spiritual?
 Why or why not?

Exercise: Follow Suit

Identify one woman who you think embodies spirituality. Pinpoint the specific characteristics or traits she displays that make you think this. Meet with her and tell her how you feel. Watch her reaction. What can you do in your life to be more like her?

Epilogue

I tried to analyze and put on paper what we women feel, think, and believe about spirituality. But the spirit of God cannot be analyzed; it can only be felt in the heart and soul.

My hope for this book is to help women, inspire them, and give hope and strength. Most important, my hope is that this book helps explain and show to the world what we women are truly about, how important our spirituality is to us, and how spirituality impacts everything in our lives.

Many women stated that the interviews were a form of catharsis for them – a clearinghouse on how they felt and thought about spirituality as well as their strength as women. One woman stated, "It was so nice to have someone talk to me about my soul and be willing to listen." My hope for this book is that it will do the same for you.

Open your souls. Touch other souls. Inspire. Make heaven on earth.

Appendix

Appendix A
To The Gentlemen, From The Ladies

"God made man and woman different. Man is not better than woman nor woman better than man. We complement each other."

Genelle

I f you had to offer advice to men about spirituality, what would you, as a woman, want to say to them? When I asked this question to the women, I requested that they respond as if they were personally communicating to all men, whether the men lived in Chicago, Seattle, Denver, Atlanta, New York or anywhere in the world.

Their responses touched me profoundly. You will feel the women's individual personalities, life experiences, and, for some, their role as mother, grandmother, mother-in-law, wife, sister or friend in their messages to the men.

We women understand that men's emotions are just as intense as ours are in the search for peace, harmony, and love in our lives. Spirituality is about depth, value, caring, and human beings. We are all bonded together and are essential to one another's spiritual journey. So, gentlemen, read with your hearts and souls and allow the women's messages to touch your souls.

Patricia: "Share it!"

Divna: "Follow your heart and your feelings. Whatever you are feeling, it is okay to discuss and to show your emotions. Who is the judge?"

Terry: "It is okay to be spiritual. Chill out. Spirituality leads to a more peaceful existence. Admit to it and your own personal calling."

Nancy: "My attraction is to men who are spiritual and who are together. It is not to men who are macho or anything else. It is that spirit I am attracted to, a man who is aware. His spirit is aware of his emotions. He doesn't shut others down. It is okay for men to cry. I don't care. I want to know all about that person. Hopefully, the package also comes nice, but it is the spirituality that they are entitled to, just as we are. It isn't just for women. It is for any being that's on earth or any other planet."

Victoria: "Before you make a judgment, walk in somebody else's shoes, because I think men are on a different level. They have to bring money home, support a family, and go up the corporate ladder. I think they are too quick to make judgment of other men or women, more so than women. It's kind of like who can outdo each other with the stories, kind of like fish stories. I feel men should walk in another man's shoes and see what it would be like to walk in their shoes, then make a statement. Then, do something. There is a God."

Cynthia: "Trust that it's okay, and give themselves permission to realize that it's okay to let go. They don't have to be in control all the time."

Nancy: "I would tell men to throw off the burdens that they carry that mask or mute that voice. Men have not been encouraged to be introspective, that is just the socialization process. Men need to know they are not in this alone. There is no reason for them to feel that they are more responsible for life than women should feel. We are all responsible and it is a lot easier doing it together than not. Throw off the responsibilities, the burdens."

Beth: "I try to teach people to be open minded. To be accepting of other people. Don't be rigid about their expectations. Have goals"

Zander: "Oh, God! That's a whole other book! Woman to man, I would tell them to stop leaning so much on themselves and this macho man thing. 'You know, I'm a man.' Tap into your spirituality. It works really great for us."

Jean: "The first thing that comes to my mind is that it's really sad that so many men truly either are afraid or just shun that part of reality. If there is any way that they could open up that little piece that's there and grow that seed, they would be a lot better off. I really think that men are threatened by it all. They are afraid. It's too feminine. It's not explainable. It goes against the nature or the essence of what little boys are taught. Things are black and white or you use words to get yourself further advanced in a company. They don't use words to be gushy and talk about their feelings. Men don't do those type of things and that's why I think that they've been sent unfairly and unjustly down a path that doesn't allow their spirituality to grow. I would hope that they could find it."

Regina: "You are a child of God. You are a unique individual. Unrepeatable! You are loved and beautiful."

Rose: "Stop being afraid of spirituality. It is not going to hurt you. I say: Accept me."

Marilyn: "It doesn't make you less of a man to care and to show that you care. I think men are real afraid of losing their macho image. Be kind. Say nice things to people. Treat other people like other human beings. There is something to be said for a man who cares and really shows that he cares. It doesn't make him less of anything. It makes him a whole lot nicer to be around."

Sally: "Not to be afraid to show spirituality."

Marge: "I don't know what advice I would give a man. I would tell my husband (deceased) I'm grateful that he followed me to church."

Virginia: "Be spiritual. Be loving. Be considerate. Understand a woman, not because she is a sex partner, or your wife, but take her for what she is, not for what you want her to be."

Sarah: "To start realizing that part of them is spiritual. I think a lot of men hunger for spirituality, but I think a lot of them are just too close-minded. They don't want to look beyond, because I think a lot of men pride themselves on being logical, scientific, but they shut themselves off. I think they are missing the boat because they are cutting a part of themselves off. They are not developing the spiritual part of themselves. They are developing themselves mentally and physically. A lot of them are into fitness, which I think is great, but I think they are missing the boat on spirituality, because I think a lot of them are very indifferent about it. They should start looking at themselves and women as spiritual beings. Maybe, to see spiritual things around them. It is okay to see God's wonders around them. Not so much as a scientific way, but as a force. As God being an energy force in creating the world and making everything around us."

Angela: "Listen to their inner selves. Don't be afraid. What we need is to get in touch with our Indian guides. We need to tap into the wisdom of the Native Americans, because they knew. Oh, yes, a very, very stratified society. There were the warriors and they needed the warriors, but they were in touch with earth, in tune with God. If I could give any advice, it would be that we need those warriors. We need those champions of businesses, but they need to feel the power of God within them. Any power a man has is not his power. Anybody's life can change with a wink of an eye. Do you know what that does to personal power? It makes us like dust on the floor when we don't tap it. Men see themselves as God's equal, not as God's sons. Men see themselves as champions of the earth, and the earth is turning. Tap in. That does not make you effeminate. It makes you more a God's child, because you acknowledge your bond."

Cindy: "To listen to the voices within."

Hope: "I know they are out there. I know there are a lot of men who have strong and powerful feelings in terms of their own spiritual beliefs. I would hope that when they are establishing their relationships with members of the opposite sex, their children, or the rest of the family, they are able to open the door and allow others to see that in them."

Kate: "Not to think spirituality is effeminate. Not to think that they would be considered wimps. Spirituality would make them stronger. It makes me stronger. It can't do anything less for them. It makes you grow in so many ways. I mean, today, the big push is for men to be in touch with their emotions and spirituality can only help. With the pressures that people have to deal with today, families, children, drugs, and crime, you can't do it on your own. Our society is not geared for someone to be totally independent. You can be, but you also work within a community, the essence of good community and self."

Kathleen: "First of all, one of the biggest problems we think of in spirituality is that the Lord God is a male, and that He is geared to males. I don't think He is. Probably, most males have a big ego and can't get into spirituality. They need to realize they need God just as much as a woman does."

Stephanie: "It is harder for men. It is harder to talk to them about spirituality. I know it is for me. When they see spirituality around them, when they see a person trying their best, men will pick it up and go on from there. I know with my own two boys, not that I talk to them that very much about it, that they do have spirituality. Somewhere along the line, they had to have picked it up. Their father, too. They had a good example."

Susan: "Believe in God! Believe in your religion. Believe in who you are."

Julianne: "I don't believe there is a whole lot of difference between men and women. There are certain differences and certain strengths, but I believe they are pretty complimentary. As long as there is communication and acceptance. Don't think of one as a flaw, as if one has strengths and one has weaknesses."

Jane: "Don't act. You have to earn spirituality. It is not something to be laughed at. It is something you can learn from. There is absolutely nothing wrong in discussing it. Spirituality doesn't show a weakness. It shows strength. It's part of the whole."

Lorraine: "I tend to think that men and women are the same. A lot of different cultural things, but ultimately down deep, we are the same – human."

Alicia: "Believe in Jesus. Believe that He is your way to your salvation. It is not being a whiny, weak, henpecked man. It's being a man. I don't think you can be a man without Him."

Toney: "To get in touch with the Lord, in order to get in touch with themselves. Do not be afraid to admit before God that they are vulnerable, but that they have some real basic needs. I would say to men and women: The Lord is the only answer. It's the only way that the man would ever be able to love his wife, as Christ loved the church. Without Him, it is impossible to love another person. Some human beings seem like they are pulling it off, but not without lasting spiritual consequences. Spirituality gives color to a black and white creature."

Kay: "Keep an open communication with God. Absolutely. As far as dealing with people, the rest of this race, no matter who they are, treat them in the way you want to be dealt with, male or female. Not just the buddy down there, the one they are having lunch with, or work with, but also the woman. Whether it's the woman who is driving the bus, or the woman who is behind the counter, or the woman sitting across the conference table with them, you know, whoever she is. I think that's where men don't look at women the same. And women are different. Don't get me wrong, but I still think we need to be treated as women. There are certain times and places, of course. I love being a woman. I think that might be where men slip up in the process of spirituality. They lose one-half of the human race over here."

Donna: "To listen. To open up. To be responsive to other things, other than what they can touch and feel and see, because there is more out there than the tangible things."

Kathy: "Let go of fear. What I find is most men are full of fear. I think, once again, society has put a burden on men to be the strong one, to be the breadwinner, to be masculine. I think so many men live with fear that they are going to be found out, because so many men don't want to admit that, even though society has told them how to act. I believe in every soul of every man that there is a desire that God has put in all of us for the spiritual growth, but fear keeps men from pursuing it. Fear of rejection from their peers. Fear that they will be considered weak. Finally, I think it is fear of what they will find out. It takes a very strong man to have a gentle heart."

Pam: "It would be for their own good to be more aware of spirituality and what they would think of spirituality. It would help their relationships."

Liz: "Own it. Share it. Don't be afraid of spirituality. You know it's interesting, because you see the feminist who talks about women's rights. They just beat the civil rights and the women's rights into the ground. I think men have also been at a disadvantage sociologically. They have had a role to play in society and that has been the role of provider, the protector, and the strong person. I don't think men have been allowed to be open, in terms of spirituality, in terms of their being emotional and in terms of sharing their feelings. I think that's where women can really help. Spirituality might not be the macho thing to do, because there really isn't any macho any more, and there really isn't any female role anymore. We are all people and we come from different orientation, like the right brain and left brain thing. There is not that structure role to play anymore."

Barbara: "To please get onto the search right away. Because I think that is the key to women reaching their full potential, that total shift now for women. I don't like to use the term liberation, but it kind of fits. Something is happening. It has been a male dominated world for thousands of years and men are having a very hard time dealing with and relating to the changes. I think if they could get in touch with their spirituality, and tap into it, they could handle the transitions so much better. It would definitely become an intertwined circle."

Martha: "To maybe not pressure themselves so much and to relax in their role as a male in society. If they are attracted to women, to not keep using beauty and polish when looking at a woman. Sort of look at the subtleties of beauty and the fact that women are people. To not worry what other people say. Men really are concerned with what people think and what their friends think. Women can sort of be their best friends."

Mary: "Acceptance and comfort with it. I think through acceptance they would allow themselves to know you. Accept it, realize that it exists and be comfortable with it."

Rita: "We are a gift. God's gift to each of us. We can be a gift to one another. God is present in each of us. God's presence comes to other people by just being who we are. And by being the best of who we are so, that we can grace other people with His presence. Each of us has contributions to this world, if we could just really trust who we are and that gift God has given us."

Irma: "Jesus is there. Just ask for Him. Pray about it. He's always there. Just knock on His door. He'll open it."

Violet: "Life is not worth living if one does not have faith in one's God, one's self and the future."

Jackie: "There is nothing wrong in being this way, going to church, feeling or crying. Men, it's okay to cry. It's okay to feel emotions. Once men realize this they will become spiritual. They think if they do this and that everybody is going to look at them as if something is wrong with them. This is going against their manhood. It's not so. There is nothing wrong with that. If they realize it, they would have better relationships. The reason men and women have this thing about communicating stems from the fact that women are so emotional and men don't understand it."

Carol: "Slow down and try to take sometime out for themselves. I never had a man who took time for himself. They are just doing, doing, doing."

Lana: "Be happy with yourself. Do things for yourself and let it benefit you and those you love. Believe in life. Try to lead a good life. Don't let fears or other people sway you, it is what you believe in. Believe and be happy with yourself."

Mari Lee: "Spirituality is wonderful. I think, most men have a difficult time tapping into the female side of their nature. They have feelings. They need to cry. They need to do all the things they think are so feminine. If they could learn to go with that, they would be a lot happier. Just become in touch with that side. There is nothing wrong with wanting to show your feelings. This macho stuff is not worth that. Everybody is human. We are all created equal. Love knows neither age nor color."

Bonnie: "I think it is different, because men are different. I would want to ask them: What do you do with your life? What motivates you?"

Evelyn: "I guess it has a lot to do with respect. I think that most men in the world that have respect and are very good had a great respect for their mothers. If you can treat other women like you would want people to treat your mother, I would say keep that in mind for relationships, because those women all have mothers. They belong to somebody. Your mother belongs to you and you belong to her. If you don't want anybody to mistreat your mother, then don't mistreat somebody else's mother or somebody else's daughter. Everybody belongs to somebody."

Anita: "I would tell men to be a little bit more outgoing with their emotions, about their feelings and about religion, because they are not. That is something men hide. If you believe in it, then that should be something you should really express, something solid, something real. Most men don't do that."

Sandra: "Men need at times in their lives somebody to lean on."

Marion: "If you don't have it, it would be helpful to belong to one of the organized religions or something else. But not to downgrade that in your life, that you were so busy that you don't have time for it. Some quiet time. That is what you need the most. Stop worrying! Sit just quietly, and let God tell you what He wants to say, instead of talking and asking Him things. Whether it's reading that helps or actual quiet time. To shut up and let Him say something to you."

Diane: "Men are human beings and have just as many claims on their spirituality. I am not sure that it can be explained in the same way as for females and that would be making us alike and that would be unfortunate, because we are not alike. We shouldn't try to categorize ourselves alike."

Ellen: "Spirituality has a lot to do with individuality. It doesn't have a lot to do with selfishness. I really think, a lot of men and a lot of women too, think of themselves first. I think for that reason they don't have it. It's sort of a matter of blending into everything. Not to lose your individuality, but strengthen it in a certain kind of way when you have that spirituality."

Mary: "Don't be afraid of it, because I think that is a barrier between men and women. Women think men are cold, heartless and unspiritual. I would say to mothers: Raise your sons in a different perspective. I don't have a son, unfortunately, but if I did, I'd raise him differently."

Karen: "Find ways to connect. Find ways to get a sense of peace."

Sue: "I think men more than women have not had the opportunity to really examine their feelings about things and to really look at some of these deep ideas, because they have been sort of pigeon-holed as much as women have and maybe more. They have been programmed to believe that they have to be a certain way and anything else should be weakness. Women have been able to be themselves, if they only wanted to or if they could let it come out. I would tell men the same thing that I would tell women. Men need to work a little harder, because their barriers are a lot thicker than ours."

Mary: "The best for men, of course, would apply to women. To be sure to choose those whom you are closest to who can help you, and you can help them. If you get in with the wrong type of person, with the wrong ideas in life, they can sometimes change your way of thinking to their way of thinking. That's not what you set out to do. When I meet someone, I don't say: Are you Catholic? Jewish? I try to accept them for who they are. Then as I learn about them a little bit later, and if I find they are doing or saying things I particularly don't like, then I don't associate with them as frequently as I would with someone I would think like. That doesn't mean they have to think as I do, because you and I can hear the same verse, or hear the same sermon, and get two different things out of it."

Francille: "The same thing for a man, especially if he is a husband, father or has a family. It is important that he have a spiritual life. It would make him a better man, have a better life."

Peggy: "Most men think they are almost too macho to have a spiritual side, not sissy exactly, but they can't be manly and be spiritual. I think you can. For a man to be spiritual makes him more of a man. I've seen so many little boys be ingrained with, don't cry. Boys aren't supposed to cry. That's wrong. I think it makes a man more of a man, and one that I can feel close to, if I know a man has emotions, like I do. It is neat for a man to express. The spirituality part and emotional part all interplay. It is real important for a man too. A man needs to understand that you can be a spiritual person and still be manly."

Karen: "There are always concerns about relationships. If a man wants a real relationship with a lady, put God first. Spirituality will come and he will have a relationship that he would never dream. Every woman, I don't care how strong they are, wants a spiritual leader. I don't care who they are. I have a girlfriend whose husband is really fixed up with the Lord. He kind of goes in spirit. When she sees him falling away, she doesn't even like him in the house. If they knew, and I could tell you men, you wouldn't believe how many kisses you would get. Kiss their whole face. It's true. If they knew, that's the key right there. The respect you feel for them, it's almost superb."

Peggy: "I would talk to men, like I do to my son-in-law: 'You have to believe, if you have a belief in God. You were raised in Catholic institutions in Mexico. They are really spiritual there. They don't miss mass. Your mother walked three to four miles to go to Mass. You have to accept God. He will take all those bad habits away from men. You have to have God.' There is no way out of it. I don't care what anybody says. That's it. Because look at me, I'm sixty-five-years-old, and I'm still going."

Marsha: I think spirituality is buried deep inside. They are afraid to let go, to show any type of emotion. There's nothing wrong with getting emotional. Men either keep their emotions so inside of them, or they rant and rave and go off the deep end the other way. There is a median. They can get in the middle of this. They can blow off steam, but they also have those emotions where they can handle crisis, too. They were brought up too macho, that it is not good for a man to cry or show any type of emotion. But they *can* show it. They are not going to be any less of a hunk or whatever you want to call it by showing that."

Christine: "Experience spirituality! It is a wonderful feeling. Don't fight it. Give in to it. Go with it. Don't be afraid of it. Make it your friend. Make it a part of you!"

Valorie: "Don't be bitter. Be more understanding. What made things go wrong in your relationship with someone, because you did find that person attractive at one time. You have to sit down and talk. The main thing is to communicate. The main thing in a relationship, and it was in mine, was money. Actually, if you sit down and talk about that, you make things better. Know what you can do without and what you can when you have it. There is a reason why things happen to people, because nobody took time out to care."

Mary Beth: "Why is it men have such a hard exterior and you can't seem to get through, even though men pretend that things don't bother them? I really think they feel a lot more stress on them because they are the breadwinners. It really bothers my husband that I make more money than he does now. Sometimes, they take on more burdens."

Nancy: "People are people. What can I tell them about spirituality? Outside of saying what I said about men and women being different because parts of their brains are different. I don't think you can differentiate between the two on spirituality. Men are just as willing to talk about spirituality as women are. They are human beings."

Ruth: "Men are spiritual. It's okay to be spiritual. Men my age (fifty) are so caught up in their machismo, their inability to share their feelings and to discuss religion. I would not be interested in a man who had no spirituality. When I get married again, and I hope I will, I would like someone to go to church with me on Sunday morning. If it's not every Sunday, it's fine, but to participate in religious activities."

Mary Jane: "Let go. Relax. Don't keep that guard up that so many men do. Come in and take a look."

Bobbie: "A man doesn't understand where a woman is coming from who has spirituality. They think you are a little neurotic, or in the change, something wrong with her, or she is not satisfied with life. A lot of men feel spirituality is a weakness. They are not going to listen, they think you are preaching, any type of individual man, white collar to blue collar."

Charlene: "I care about you. Take care of yourselves. Love yourself. Respect yourself. Walk with your Higher Power."

Rosetta: "Find religion or find that inner feeling. Be more understanding. Be more considerate. Be there for you."

Zenaida: "Whoever, live it! Life is so important. Sooner or later you find out what the meaning is."

Ginny: "To be more open about it. I don't know why. My boys are not quite as religious as I am. To not be afraid of it. It's almost like they think they are not macho or they think they can't do it on their own. It would probably help them a lot if they express themselves that way. I really try hard with my boys, because their friends believe that's not the way to be."

Joan: "Find spirituality, bring it out. Use it, especially in a relationship, a meaningful relationship with a woman. Bring it out. Share it during a relationship."

Nancy: "It is very personal and you need to pray by yourself. Feel that comfortableness. Just take the prayer of serenity and use that as the biggest part of your life. There are things that you just have to turn over. You can't carry baggage. You can't. You have to let the baggage go. That is the most wonderful thing about prayer, it allows you to let go. Move on and start all over again, as long as you are sincere."

Carol: "Just open your mind to spirituality, to that possibility of it. The need to listen."

Gerry: "I would not volunteer advice. I would not. Only if they were reaching out. I don't think anyone could hear, if they don't want to hear."

Leah: "We have made life confusing for men. They don't know what they should say or what they shouldn't say. When they should hold the door open and when they shouldn't. When they should cry and when they shouldn't cry. So a lot of that should be dismissed. They should also be comfortable with themselves. If you are a rugged person, male or female, that is you. Don't velvet glove yourself. If you are an awfully soft person, there may not be a need to become tougher. You can learn how to do what you want to do with what you are. I think more often than not, society has been unfair to men. It's made them tougher. I think you can catch a lot of bees with honey, and women in that sense, probably have had more control than anyone has wanted to acknowledge. You can do a lot by making the other person think they can do it. Whereas men, unfortunately have been trained by society to do this, and to do that. Women have been able to be more subtle and get things done."

Denise: "Men would have a better understanding of women. Internalize it more. Focus inward. Internal is more important then external. Spirituality is very important for relationships with men; to recognize each other, because we are going to be very different that way and to say: It's okay that we are different. I like you because of this."

Jennifer: "It is important in any relationship that they both have spirituality so men and women can communicate. Part of spirituality is being comfortable with yourself and who you are. Before people can connect with other people, they need to know who they are. Sometimes, men need to get away from this macho thing. Sometimes, when they let their defenses down a little bit more, they see more of themselves."

Annette: "To get their heads in gear and find spirituality. There was an article in the paper just last weekend that the majority of people who go to church are women and elderly. I don't know why men won't recognize spirituality. I think they think it isn't macho, maybe, because they think God is another man. I try to rationalize why. Men should talk more to other men about their feelings and I think their spirituality will show through. I don't think men talk to men enough. Nobody wants to be first to admit that they have inner fears or that their faith or spirituality can help. I don't know what they fear, but I think they have fears."

Erna: "I tell you to change your habits. Some of them swear too much, smoke too much, drink too much, chase around too much and gamble too much. They have all kinds of bad habits, but I would say change your habits. Get down on your knees and ask the Lord to help you. That's all I would tell them."

Alice: "They should find a woman who they think is spiritual. Men can access it through women more than they can through themselves. I really think that they need a female counterpart for that."

Ruth: "Do what the Lord wants. If you are married, love your wife."

Mary: "It could really solve a lot of the problems that they have in their lives, if they just yield to God and do what He would have them do. It could settle their roamings, their minds, their confusions. It could just make everything in life better for them. They are not going to find it out around other places. They go to the bars, they drink and still think they are going to find all this peace and wonderful good times, not to mention the things they are going to have. That's not going to do it. Only God can do it."

Ellin: "We forget that delicate relationship with women and people. I would ask them to slow down and tell the truth and take some time to do some introspective things."

Julianne: "To get some spirituality."

Ellen: "The world is not a place to be by yourself. You might make it, but you are going to do it the hard way. It never hurts to have a little help. I believe that you should look. Do something that will always be there. You will never be abandoned. You can always depend on it. I would reiterate that you are not giving up anything, you are gaining everything."

Carol: "Not to be afraid of spirituality. Listen to their inner knowledge."

Eugenia: "Not to be afraid to be sensitive to spiritual things. It's not unmanly to realize that it is an important thing to your wife or your children and who you go home to. No matter how good your relationship is, I really think it can get better, both to the intimacy and also the physical. To be there. To have spirituality. Cohesive."

Lisa: "Spirituality isn't a real male thing. Each and every one of them should explore it. If a man would explore into it, he would be quite an unique human being. All human beings have unique qualities about them, so I guess I would say: Don't be afraid to look for the unique qualities that you have and the unique learning experiences you might gain. If there is a situation in your life, you should try to learn from it, because I think you gain spirituality from your experiences."

Kerry: "To find spirituality. I mean to really understand that it is not just practicing religion, but that it is really something deep inside. It's okay. To me, spirituality is part of what makes us cry. It helps us to be emotional. Whether it makes us emotional, I don't know. It is very hard for men, I think, to cry."

Kathy: "I think it's a woman's issue. I think men are raised to have this feeling of taking care of themselves and being inner tough. Most men I know to some degree say: I have to take care of myself. I need to pull from myself, I need to be number one, and take care of myself. Some are better than others. If I would give them advice, they probably would look at me and say: Who do you think you are? I'm probably a little chauvinistic myself to say, but it's my honest answer."

Nancy: "Don't try to be so strong. Same thing as for women. Don't fight it. Listen. Let go! I think when this is all over, I don't think there is really much difference between men and women as far as how they handle things. It's society saying: Little boys shouldn't cry and little boys shouldn't do this. That's wrong."

Di: "I know they have a hard time being brought up the way they were. You know, especially in that generation, their values, what they were supposed to be as part of a man."

Genelle: "Men have an awesome responsibility, because God has given them the world of being superior or being in control. As my father-in-law used to say about his wife: 'I may be the head, but she's the neck.' I thought that was such wisdom from him because he respected her so. He felt he was the one to make the decisions, but he felt she was an integral part of the decisions. He always asked her for advice. So therefore, I have a husband from that example that I'm very much part of the decisions. I would say to men: Don't look at your position of being Lord or the boss. Look at your position as a leader. A leader should lead by example. For a man to be more spiritual, he should be the word. He should let it permeate his life, so that how he walks is the same as how he talks. Be in the word. Listen to other people. Learn as much as you can. As an expression, I heard if you want to get to the top, see how many people you can take with you. That is spirituality!"

Jo: "First word that comes to me is partner. Partners in the growth, and that it is funny, because immediately what's surfacing for me are images of people in my life. So, I don't see that giant world that you describe in telling men out there or very specific men. Just saying: Our contributions are equally important."

Molly: "Share advice. Do not be afraid to do that. The power is within all of us. Men have been cheated because, for the most part, our society hasn't allowed them that, and telling them it's not okay for them to be spiritual. It just hasn't been."

Jan: "When he is touching my skin, or when he is really into my head, that he is connected with my soul, and be careful. Be careful. Men, collectively, I would want to say to value your defenses and to relate to me as a whole person. I want him to come to me as a whole person. Let us share at that level. Collectively, the whole idea of macho, the whole idea of being strong, being in charge, and in control, I like that to a big extent. But also the realization, they find somebody they can really trust in an unconditional kind of living relationship. It's okay to share their insecurities."

Jenae: "Don't be afraid of women and that energy and their power."

Susan: "Don't hold in their feelings. Not to think that there is some mental picture of what a man is. Just be a person. Think of other people that way as well. They would be better off. There is no old boys network, and I know there is, but that this would be a better world if there weren't and we were all equals. Living in an urban area, I see a lot of men who treat women like equals. But traveling throughout the country and even other countries, I know that women are not treated as equals throughout the country. It hurts them. Some of it is that women set up their own barrier to who they want to be. A lot of that is due to men constantly telling women they are not good enough to make their own decisions, and that they need to allow men to take care of them and tell them what's best for them. So I would tell men to just allow themselves to be who they are, without thinking of being man or woman, or masculine identity, but just learn more about themselves and go with their feelings."

Elaine: "You are God."

Appendix B
A Final Word With The Ladies

"You are a child of God. You are a unique spiritual being. You are beautiful!"

Regina

I f you had to offer advice to other women about spirituality, what would you want to say to them? When I asked this question to the one hundred women, I asked them to respond as if they were personally communicating to all women, whether the women lived in California, the Dakotas, the Midwest, Georgia, Vermont, or anywhere in this magnificent world.

The women's responses are in the form of personal messages to each and every one of you who has this book in your hands right now. The messages come from the hearts and souls of the one hundred women and therefore are presented verbatim.

Patricia: "Plant your own garden. Decorate your own soul. Do the things in your life to make it happen."

Divna: "It starts from yourself. It is very important to find time daily to put aside for yourself. There is no one universal recipe, because all of us are individuals. Whatever works for you. Soft music, yoga, reading to yourself, your own time, even if it is closing the bathroom door to shave your legs. Try to be independent, because that makes one feel secure and connected with the universe."

Terry: "Spirituality is there if you want it. The biggest thing is that you have to want it. If you don't want it, then it is not there and accepting it will not be achieved easily. Things have to occur in our lives to where we evolve to it, and then when that period comes, do not be afraid."

Nancy: "Accept yourself. Claim what is your God given right. Claim your own personal power, that part of you that is you. Accept it, love it, and realize that you deserve to be happy. See it as something now and that you are happy now. Right in this moment and you are going to fly with it. Even if you have to tell yourself so many times an hour, I am happy, whether you believe it or not. When you decide that you are going to be happy, things will go right in your life and you will look at what is going on around you. You become aware. You then see there are so many avenues of choice. So many avenues of joy. You initially have to accept."

Victoria: "Believe in yourself. Have faith that there is God and He will help you do what you need to do."

Cynthia: "Spirituality is your source of comfort. It will be your comforter when you are by yourself, your source of strength. It will give you guidance and direction. You will never feel like you are completely alone and that you have no resources or no place to turn. If you trust and believe, you'll have joy in the midst of sorrow. Happiness is transient, but joy comes from within. It will see you through all of your rough times. It will withstand. It will."

Nancy: "Have enough faith in yourself to respect what it is that your inner self is saying. Listen to that voice and believe in that voice, because it's your voice. Once you get to that point, you will see that the rest is not that tough. If you can come back and say, I am answering something that I have within myself, regardless of how that voice got there. That voice might have gotten there, because as I am inclined to believe, it was there at the beginning. Or that you were turned in certain ways, and that's where your values come from, or that you had some sort of episode, event, make those words with, regardless of how it came. That voice is yours. Value it."

Beth: "I try to teach people to be open minded. To be accepting of other people. Don't be rigid about their expectations. Have goals."

Zander: "I would tell them that, we as women, have to trust there is a higher place when life deals unfair blows. There is a higher place. There is something bigger than we are. It will really jump out at you."

Jean: "To feel free to explore spirituality. That is the most important. There's going to be people who are going to say: 'You're wrong. That isn't true. Why are you doing that? Are you a Bible fanatic?' But again intuition should talk. It always talks and you should listen to it. Explore it the best you can, by going to church or by joining one-on-one Bible readings. Live your spirituality. Not just think about it, but act on it."

Regina: "You are a child of God. You are a unique spiritual being. You are beautiful!"

Rose: "It is something that you follow. It is something you have to enhance. Do it in whichever way you feel is best. I can get my Bible and read a verse or two and I am totally different. Totally different. It is like the weight has been lifted. Like the barrier has been broken. It is like nobody can touch you now. You are sitting on top of the world."

Marilyn: "You can't force spirituality on people. You have to find it yourself. What is right for me may not be right for you. I can set an example. I can take you to church with me. I can get you involved with the choir. If it is not right for you, I can't make you stay and I wouldn't want to. So, you have to find yourself."

Sally: "Draw from wherever you feel it is coming from. Chill out. Then bring spirituality into your life to make it better. To make someone else's life better."

Marge: "We have to hang in there, and when you think that there isn't anyone listening to what you have to say, know that there is someone out there. It might take a while, but eventually it comes. And like I said, I found that out first hand."

Virginia: "You have to like yourself first. If you like yourself, you like other people. You will know when these people are good and honest. Be your own strength and everything else comes. I don't care if you are poor or rich, if you have your strength, you will have everything."

Sarah: "Women have to realize who they are as women. What their gifts are. God gave them certain beautiful gifts. We are more emotional, which, I think, makes us more understanding about human life and problems. I think as a whole, women are more compassionate. They need to appreciate one another. To associate with one another. To tell each other that they are loved and appreciated, but also to tell men as well. They need to set time aside to meditate. To be within themselves. To find out who they are and to know what God wants of them. To hear God speak to them through them. They need to see God's wonders in things around them. Simple things, like taking a walk in the forest, looking at the leaves changing in the fall, watching snow fall, watching drops of rain fall on a leaf of a tree, watching birds as they fly. Just appreciating nature around them. That is important, because those are simple things that we all can see no matter where we live."

Angela: "To recognize the spirituality with themselves, because the minute they recognize the spirituality with themselves, they have also found their strength. Once you find your strength, you can detach, emotionally, from all the chains that have been holding you bound. Most women are economically dependent on a man, but that doesn't mean I have to be emotionally dependent on a man. Economical dependency does not mean servitude, it means partnership. Most women have exchanged something and have given their mates something in return for their economical dependence. Whether it is to be the mother of children, whether to be a helpmate in a business, or just to be a helpmate in a home. That doesn't make a woman a second class citizen. The minute a woman gets in touch with her spirituality she has found her strength. Strength doesn't mean the ability to bring home a six-figure income. Strength means to be able to look at a situation, for what it is worth, and do the best you can, in spite of all odds."

Cindy: "To listen to the voices within."

Hope: "Spirituality is so important to me. It is something that I would hope everyone would have, but I know they don't. It would help them in their lifestyles, wherever they are. It certainly helps to adjust your priorities and deal with things on a much better level. I would hope they could find something like that along the line."

Kate: "Not to think religion or spirituality is a cop out, because a lot of people in my generation used to think that if you relied on your faith, it was just not facing your problems. It is not that at all. Spirituality is talking with God and listening to what He has to say. It is facing your problems in a completely different way, in a much freer way. Actually in a more truer way to yourself. Those problems are there. Life is not without problems. God gives you problems. You create your problems. When you let go, and work with God to solve those problems, it is so much easier."

Kathleen: "Part of spirituality is union. It is a help for someone to lean on. It is some way to continue going and growing. It is a reward. If you don't have a background of spirituality, the communion with God, then growth becomes really stagnant. You can't look back. You have to look forward. And the only way to do it, is to ask help from above. If I didn't have it, I wouldn't be where I am at this point."

Stephanie: "Believe in God, because He is always there for you. You are going to get that strength. He is there for you whenever you need Him. Yet some of us may not think it. Maybe God did not answer what we want. Somewhere along the line He's there for you. No matter what!"

Susan: "Believe in God! Believe in your religion. Believe in who you are."

Julianne: "Go where it is most comfortable for you. Go in the direction of comfort and the path, but not of least resistance. Because resistance makes you stronger. Don't take anyone's word on what is right or what is wrong for you. Because everyone is an individual. There are no rules as far as spirituality is concerned."

Jane: "Be happy. There is nothing wrong with it. There is nothing wrong in believing. It's truth. Truth is you, because it is part of you."

Lorraine: "It is not something you can really have overnight and wake up one morning and decide that it's there. It's God that comes through."

Alicia: "I would like them to know that the Lord loves you, no matter what a man tells you abut yourself that is not true. God chose women in very strong parts of the Bible. He used women in ways that He couldn't use a man, because He knows that we are better at accomplishing things. He had a woman Deborah lead a war. Come on! We can't even let men allow us to be in an army. Deborah was an infantry man and she guided them. She was the person who communicated with God and with the army. She was not a man, but a woman. Don't ever let a man say, 'Well, God said you will have a painful birth, or you are to follow in a man's route or that you are not intelligent.' That is not true."

Toney: "If you are in a position where you are afraid that becoming a believer in Jesus Christ, belonging to Him, is going to make you less of a woman, less of a person, don't believe that. It is not so. Don't think that by becoming the servant you are less of a person. Jesus didn't say that only the woman to become the servant. He said: 'Man and woman to become servants to each other.' There is a lot you can't realize about Christianity until you make that step a real personal one. You trusted God with your life. Let Him show you, if you are a listener!"

Kay: "Keep an open communication with God, that is a big one. Try to always be honest with yourself. The big teaching of Christ is: 'Doing to others, what you would have done to you.' You know when you walk that way, it makes a difference."

Donna: "Just to be true to their God and to be true to themselves. Because, you don't have answers. Nobody knows what is going on but God and you. You have to answer for that at some point. Plus your conscience has to deal with that for the rest of your life."

Kathy: "I had to find it out the hard way. When I was in a tremendous amount of turmoil, I had looked to everybody for my answer. I looked to the church, I looked to my friends, my relatives. I even went to a psychic and psychotherapists. I looked to everybody else to solve my problems except me. It comes from within. God has given us guides, guardian angels, and spiritual leaders to help us find the answers from within. But very few people know how to tap into the source that is available to us. The concept is very far-fetched for most people. If you talk to somebody about a spiritual guide, they immediately think the girl has gone off the deep end. If we could spend fifteen minutes a day in quiet meditation it would change our lives. Fifteen minutes a day in not a lot of time to spend to change our lives. The problem is people don't know how to meditate. They fall asleep. Their minds wander and then they say it doesn't work. That's okay. Learning meditation is like learning anything else. It takes time. When you try to learn to ride a bicycle, you fall off, but you get back on. Meditation is something that takes time. But eventually if you could spend fifteen minutes a day in quiet meditation, simply opening yourself to receive what God has for you, every answer will come to you. You don't have to get it from anybody else, but sitting there and waiting for it from within. That is something."

Pam: "To let it flow and trust in God. Be aware of His power and His presence. Take time everyday to try to get closer go Him."

Liz: "Own it! Take it and win it. It's yours! Be proud of it. Share it. Make a difference! I think women don't own their power or take responsibility for their own spirituality. I think it's because they haven't had the opportunity. If you look back at your ancestors in the United States, these were the settlers and they had ten kids, so they could have enough kids to work on the farm. Life was about survival. In so many cases, that's what life was about: survival and reproduction. But now, all of the technological advancements, and the Industrial Revolution, and all this technology of the twentieth century, in the world for everybody, we have to own our spirituality. Otherwise we won't raise the consciousness. We won't save the earth and we won't fight world hunger."

Barbara: "It is the most important part of a person. No matter what you are doing with your goals and accomplishments, it is always the power you are working on. You will find that the rest of your life. It will all fall into place. Center on that, no matter what else you are doing."

Martha: "You can only develop your spirituality by really taking time for yourself and actually being alone for a good deal of time. You can't kid yourself about it. You shouldn't try to be and do everything. You should try to close the magazines, as far as your portrayal of women, and get a grip on who and what you want to be. It is more about inner strength. Take yourself away from anything that will bring you down and be aware of it. Why kid yourself. We are living, breathing animals. Your body needs special things."

Mary: "Have faith. Have faith in God. A complete trust. Just total focus on it!"

Rita: "We are a gift. God's gift to each of us. We can be a gift to one another. God is present in each of us. God's presence comes to other people by just being who we are. And by being the best of who we are so, that we can grace other people with His presence. Each of us has contributions to this world, if we could just really trust who we are and that gift God has given us."

Irma: "Jesus is there. Just ask for Him. Pray about it. He's always there. Just knock on His door. He'll open it."

Violet: "Life is not worth living if one does not have faith in one's God, one's self and the future."

Jackie: "Don't feel afraid to discuss spirituality. Don't be afraid to feel it. Sometimes people can say things and make you say: 'Maybe I should back up, because maybe I shouldn't feel this way or say these things.' It's okay to feel the way you feel, because other women are feeling the same way. It is people that you meet. They have this energy. You will actually see it and it makes you feel good. It makes you say: 'Here, it is worth it. I'm not alone feeling this.' It does exist. That's the most. It feels good to know the way you feel in your heart, that you are not alone and God is letting you know it is right to feel this way. He is showing this is the way to feel. It is goodness."

Carol: "Just be the best you can be, because in bad times you have to be strong. It's important."

Lana: "Be happy with yourself. Do things for yourself and let it benefit you and those you love. Believe in life. Try to lead a good life. Don't let fears or other people sway you, it is what you believe in. Believe and be happy with yourself."

Mari Lee: "I think we all know the difference between good and evil. The answers to any questions that you have are right inside you. If you go the right way, you are going to be rewarded. You are going to see that going the wrong way is not good. It goes back to the same thing, what goes around, comes around. We all know what we really should do. We just have to be smart enough to do what is right with us, because we all have all the answers right inside of us. Sometimes we need something to help pull them out of us."

Bonnie: "To ask yourselves if you are happy or aren't happy, and if you know why. And then ask yourselves what it was you were lacking and if you didn't know what it is, find out."

Evelyn: "I would tell women, especially first and foremost, to gain respect! Respect yourself. You have to head up your own world. You have to live by what you know in your heart is right. If you don't show respect for yourself, then you can't demand respect from anybody else. I think men see this when they look at women, or people in general. The way you carry yourself says a lot about you. You can take one look and see the way a woman is. Even dress shows a certain amount of how she respects herself. The company she keeps and the things that she does. The routines she has. It says a lot about that person. It doesn't necessarily mean that she is a terrible person, inwardly, because she might be hiding to overcome some of these things. But, if you can display a certain amount of respect for yourself, that without a doubt, is vibrating off of everybody else. Then, I know you can demand respect. It's beautiful."

Anita: "Don't be afraid!"

Sandra: "When you are alone, you do have God to watch over you. He's always there when you need Him."

Marion: "If you don't have it, it would be helpful to belong to one of the organized religions or something else. But not to downgrade that in your life, that you were so busy that you don't have time for it. Some quiet time. That is what you need the most. Stop worrying! Sit just quietly, and let God tell you what He wants to say, instead of talking and asking Him things. Whether it's reading that helps or actual quiet time. To shut up and let Him say something to you."

Diane: "Don't be afraid of it. But I would like to know more about it. We should. There are different levels, the metaphysical, mental, physical, emotional, and spiritual. I would like definitions of all of those for myself, as well. That is how you learn as a person and think of them in those terms, and whatever these definitions are. That would be wonderful. That would be knowing people. And knowing yourself."

Ellen: "Don't be afraid to be an individual. Be yourself, regardless of what other people think. I guess, all my life, I have marched to my own drummer, and that is what I think that other people should do. It is very difficult, because people get caught in all kinds of things. When you are in a relationship situation, you find yourself doing things that you might not have done under other circumstances, because it is an entirely different balance or situation."

Mary: "Spirituality exists! Explore things and you will find more to be spiritual about. A lot of that is seeking out other women. You just can't get it all alone. I mean, you can read, meditate, or go to church if you have one, or lectures at the university. Just become as knowledgeable as you can. Be enough of a person and listen."

Karen: "Find ways to connect. Find ways to get a sense of peace."

Sue: "To be able to identify your spirituality adds such a dimension to your life. It is such a good feeling to have about yourself. To be able to say: 'This is who I am!' I am not trying to say I'm by myself. I think my religion, my belief in God, and all those other kind of things are real parts, but this is part of the core. It's not separate from it, it is part of it. I think it is always there. It is never separate. It is finally being able to see it there, and you don't have to go to school to do that. You don't have to have a faith of profession. There are no prerequisites. It's there! All you have to do is give yourself a chance to see it. Let it come out. Not to be afraid to do it."

Mary: "Try to find out what you are striving for, what you want to believe in, and what you think is there that you can grasp to make your own life better. I have hardly known of anyone who took on anything like that, that didn't feel better about themselves or others."

Francille: "If you want contentment in life, if you want to feel success in life and feel that you have accomplished something, you have to be spiritual. I don't see any other way."

Peggy: "Every woman should make a supreme effort to achieve spirituality whether, it be the spirit of a woman, or spirituality, or oneness with God, or religion. I just think it is so important for a woman to have. Not just a woman, but anybody. But maybe especially to a woman because we have to deal with so much more. I think all women should make an effort to have a spiritual side to them that they can tap into."

Karen: "Seek the kingdom of God first, and everything they want in their life will be added to them. Psalm thirty-seven, verse four: 'Delight yourself in the Lord and He would give you the desires of your heart.' Praise Him, thank Him, serve Him, ask Him, and the spirituality will come and their whole life will change. He wants to give us the desires of our heart. We are His children and all we have to do is praise Him. First we praise, then we thank, and then we ask. It will change you, but it might not change the world around you. If nothing else, the circumstances may be the same, but you'll be different."

Peggy: "Accept Jesus Christ. You need God to raise your children nowadays. You do. Because there is nothing there if you don't. He will be your whole life. You have to accept Him, to be completely your whole life. You can't leave anything out to become completely in Christ."

Marsha: "Everybody has the inner strength in them, but you don't know it because it is buried inside of you by someone else's feelings, such as, you can't do that. So, you look down on yourself. I think you have to realize that, first of all, you are a person. Be true to yourself. You have to make yourself happy before you can make anybody else happy. You have to just try and find it. You have to say to yourself that you are a strong person and you can handle little situations and gradually build yourself up. I think everybody has it, whether it is a lot or a little, but it is how you open yourself up to it, that it is there or not."

Christine: "Experience spirituality! It is a wonderful feeling. Don't fight it. Give in to it. Go with it. Don't be afraid of it. Make it your friend. Make it a part of you!"

Valorie: "Not to be bitter, because it reflects on yourself. People say to me: 'Why aren't you bitter?' If I were, I would see wrong in everybody, even in children. Kids are kids! They can be irritating at times, but if you look at them, they are just learning and bitterness can't be."

Mary Beth: "Spirituality does not necessarily mean that you will have an easier life, but it provides such a peace about things, that you might come across a life you want."

Nancy: "One of the great things I have learned is to stop giving advice. This is my part of the world, my spirituality."

Ruth: "To try hard. Definitely to look forward to finding it."

Mary Jane: "It is not hard to find. But it is hard to realize you have it. You are not quite sure what it is, but it is just this inner feeling you have over life and values and of everything. Once you find it, once you realize you have it, don't let go. Keep developing and nurturing it."

Bobbie: "It is a personal thing. When you feel this feeling, you'll know it. You'll feel it. If you want to have it or if you are looking for it, then it's time. Reach out. It will find you. You have to do it unselfishly. You can't be looking for something in return."

Charlene: "Be yourself. You are a precious being. You need to love yourself."

Rosetta: "Listen to your inward feeling and how you feel about it. Follow it."

Zenaida: "Spirituality is something you have to learn."

Ginny: "The most important thing is to live it. Really. It is not how often you go to church or what church. It's just you really have to live it. It really helps to get you through. But you have to pray within your heart and He will really help you. But actually you are helping yourself. It's just something you can feel. You really can."

Joan: "I think everybody has spirituality. I think you have to look for it. You have to want to find it. You need to search yourself. Search your soul. I think being alone helped me do that. I had nobody around me and that's when I decided I am going to get on. I am going to find out what I am all about. I was very lonely after my divorce, and I was scared, but only for a short period in time. Then I just decided okay, these are the cards that were dealt; now I am going to handle it."

Nancy: "It is very personal and you need to pray by yourself. Feel that comfortableness. Just take the prayer of serenity and use that as the biggest part of your life. There are things that you just have to turn over. You can't carry baggage. You can't. You have to let the baggage go. That is the most wonderful thing about prayer, it allows you to let go. Move on and start all over again, as long as you are sincere."

Carol: "Can't buy it! Can't go shopping for it. It is something that needs to be developed. It really has to come from each person from within. I don't think it is something that anybody can give to you or that you can purchase."

Gerry: "The spirituality or the feeling you have that helps you get through the day, get through life, the tough spots, the belief that there is. I believe in an after-life. I believe that what you are doing, it doesn't have to be perfect all the time, but that it is important. Helps you cope. It's something that is just there. My belief in God. My belief that you can get closer to a situation if you just think it through and pray for guidance. It's worked."

Leah: "Probably enforcing what we thought about in the sixties. Believe in yourself. You are wonderful. You are beautiful. You are brilliant. There is nothing you can't do. Go. Fight. If you fail, do it again. Don't let anybody ever tell you that you can't do anything."

Denise: "I think when you talk about barriers, I think that is part of it. There is always one to overcome. To believe in yourself. No one else will. Especially in today's world, women are still so discriminated against and even amongst each other. Women are worse enemies towards each other at times. It's not callous or rude to be thinking about yourself."

Jennifer: "Spirituality is at different levels for each person. I think everybody needs some spirituality. Everybody has to draw on something. Where you get it depends on you. I like doing it in church too, even with the singing. It's just a positive thing going to church and that helps. Everybody has their own comfort level. Their own A to Z and where they fit into the spectrum.

Are they going to go a one hundred percent? One thousand percent? Or are they standing a little further back?"

Annette: "You can't have spirituality by yourself. You need to share it. Find it with someone. Having friends or a friend. You need someone like that. I don't know too many people that have spirituality and are lovers. Anyone who I have known that is truly spiritual is always giving of themselves. Yes, I truly believe that."

Erna: "Just have faith in the Lord, that's all you need. A lot of people will say it's hogwash, but to me, it isn't. If it wasn't for my faith, I don't know where I'd be. I really don't. That's my life – my Lord!"

Alice: "It helps to belong to a universal group and to really feel that bond with women around the world. Even though our situations are different, we are really going through a lot of the same thing. Just to feel that there are enough people out there going through it and tap into it."

Ruth: "I'm not good at giving advice. Everything is by the purity and knowledge of knowing that the Lord is your Savior. Recognize it. Accept it. So many people know it but won't accept it. You are able to bring Him back in your life, when you say I'm ready now. That's when the spirituality really flows."

Mary: "It could be the most important thing in your life. It is something to strive for. It helps to insulate the people around you. Stability. It gives you roots, just like a tree. If you get settled good, and you know what you really believe in, you won't let people sway you. Maybe they don't believe like you do. Hey, there is no one church that's going to get you to heaven. It is going to be for everybody. God is whites, reds, yellows and blacks. So when we live in this world, we need to get along together. As far as our stability and Christianity and all, we need to dig our roots deeper and be more sure of ourselves."

Ellin: "In nature there is a masculine and feminine, just as there is spirituality. I mean, we are talking about matter here. There is this and there is this. We don't really think as in view of spirit. You know, however, we look at a sunset and we see them in view of spirit. I feel one of the great losses of our world is that we don't recognize spirit in everything we are."

Julianne: "As hard as the right choices are most of the time, do make them, because in the long run, you will be a much happier person. You will feel much better about yourself."

Ellen: "The world is not a place to be by yourself. You might make it, but you are going to do it the hard way. It never hurts to have a little help. I believe that you should look. Do something that will always be there. You will never be abandoned. You can always depend on it. I would reiterate that you are not giving up anything, you are gaining everything."

Carol: "Not to be afraid of spirituality. There is, in fact, something here that we don't understand, but it can give meaning to your life."

Eugenia: "Get down to brass tacks with God and be honest. I think God appreciates honesty more than anything else. It's kind of what I believe has helped my own unbelief. God, I really do want to know You. I really want to trust You, but I want to know. You show me how. Whatever it takes. These are risky statements. It is not a list of do this and do this and this. There are some things that can help, but it doesn't really get you there."

Lisa: "Never quit looking for spirituality. When you quit looking for it, or quit wanting it, something happens to you. I don't think it's anything that is good, but I think good things come to you when you try."

Kerry: "Seek it out. Find it. Nurture it."

Kathy: "Spirituality is something that you work on every day. I guess you really need to be conscious of it. You can pull from a lot of different resources and people to help develop it and keep it alive. Religion is a vital part of it. If you have that consistently in your life, it's giving you different ways of dealing with things, because life itself can be so hard, it can take away so much of your strength. But if you can get it back through religion, it builds you back up again. You need that to keep building, and working on it, and giving you more and more inner strength."

Nancy: "Don't fight it! Just listen to it. And let go."

Di: "Spirituality is out there. Don't go searching for it. It will happen, if you want it bad enough. But you can't go out there and say: 'Well, I'm going to go get spiritual now.' It just happens through different experiences and different mistakes. I think that's good. Let it try to happen to you or maybe seek somebody that you feel is spiritual. Maybe ask them how they get their spirituality."

Genelle: "Do what makes you feel good and makes you healthy. I think spirituality has to do with your physical health. It makes you happy. When you are radiating a spiritual being from you, it makes you at peace, comforting."

Jo: "First, try to understand and connect to some kind of love. Whatever the definition is for that individual. Try to listen to the intuition, and that will be a beginning. I do feel strongly about support groups. I would define a group as two or more. And listen to the intuition. I need to say, 'I am a very well educated western industrialized person.' I think my spiritual direction is very different from someone who is a peasant on a farm in a third world country. I do believe that I have a lot more trappings to my spiritual direction. I have a lot more work to do, in terms of trying to get through to clarity and to my mission."

Molly: "Listen within yourself, the voice within. Because that's where you find truth. That is where you will find other power, or that inner power, or your best power. But it is within! The only way to hear is to use silence. Take time away so that you can really hear."

Jan: "As women we get caught up in the whole area of doing so much. We are valued by doing, whether it's in the home, as a mother and a wife, or as a career woman. We value by doing. One thing I've let slowly sink in is the whole value of just being. The value that I am just because I am, and not because of what I am per se. Just the value of deep down realizing the consciousness of God within. I would encourage women to slow down enough, and be in touch with who they are as a being, rather then just what they can do."

Jenae: "Find a little corner in your room or some space you can call your own, if it's three feet by three feet, or if it's a closet. Put, whether it's a box or a beautiful antique dresser, or things that are special to you, a candle or whatever in this room. Discipline yourself, to sit down for ten minutes a day and just be quiet. You are very valuable to everybody, because of what's inside of you!"

Susan: "To be themselves! The thing that frustrates me about so many women is that they are waiting for somebody else to make the decision for them. To lead them down the path. To tell them what to do and why. I want to tell them to be who they are, and feel good about who they are, and know that. I am speaking of spiritual goodness of people. We all have a lot to offer one another. The more we reach our own potential, the more we can give to society and make this a better place to live. Be themselves! Not to listen to what other people tell them, but to do what it is they want to do in life."

Elaine: "The same thing I told the men: You are God."

Appendix C

Meet the Ladies

"Spirituality is the common thread that binds us together with other women, to mankind, and to the universal light – God."

Michelle

From Alabama:

Nancy, 47, Married
Caucasian
Registered Nurse,
Mother, Wife
Methodist, then
Baptist for past
twenty-six years

From Alaska:

Elaine, 43, Married
Caucasian
Psychologist
Practice through
Siddha Meditation

From California:

Carol, 35, Married
Caucasian
Customer Service,
Mother, Wife
Methodist all her life

From Colorado:

Carol, 38, Divorced
Caucasian
Director of Human
Resources
No religious affiliation

Carol, 48, Married
Caucasian
Childhood Educator,
Artist
Traditional Native
American Indian

Di, 39, Married
Caucasian
Staff Assistant for
Child Care Education
Mother, Wife
Roman Catholic all
her life

Ellen, 47, Married
Caucasian
Director of Head
Start Program for
Children Services
Presbyterian, then
Nazarene for past
fifteen years

Ellin, 40, Married
Caucasian
Producer of Audio/
Visual Tapes for
Children, Mother
Christian and not
practicing a specific
religion

Eugenia, 57,
Married
Caucasian
Nutrition Consultant
with a USDA Child
Care Pre-Program
Protestant
Non-Denominational
for the past ten years

Genelle, 49,
Married
Caucasian, Native
American Indian
Child of God,
Wife, Mother
Nutrition Consultant
Church of Christ all
her life

Jan, 51, Single
Caucasian
Executive Director of
Child Care Services
Mother
Christian all her life

Jo, 41, Married
Caucasian
Executive Director of
Non-Profit Regional
Center
Methodist all her life

Julianne, 41, Married
Caucasian
Mother, Homemaker
Food Program Consultant
Catholic and not formally
practicing

Kathy, 32, Married
Caucasian
Owner of Day Care
Center, Consultant for
Food Program
Mother, Wife
Roman Catholic, then
Non-Denomination for
past five years

Kerry, 41, Divorced
Caucasian
Director of Child Care
Institutions and
Resources at Community
College
Baptist, then Mormon for
past twelve years

Lisa, 31, Married
Caucasian, Native
American Indian
Coordinator of Day
Care Center, Admin-
istrative Assistant
Lutheran and open to
all religions

Molly, 44, Married
Caucasian
Administrator of
School Age Child
Care Programs and
Training
Roman Catholic all
her life

Nancy, 38, Married
Caucasian
Director of Child
Care Food Programs,
Wife, Mother
Presbyterian, then
Church of Christ for
past three years

From Georgia:

Barbara, 31, Single
Caucasian
Office Administrator
Roman Catholic, then
Non-Denomination
for past ten years

Donna, 29, Married
African American
Service Manager

Methodist, then
Presbyterian for past
twenty-four years

Kathy, 41, Divorced
Caucasian
Teacher
Christian all her life

Kay, 37, Married
Caucasian
Marketing Coordinator,
Mother, Wife
Christian all her life

Liz, 30, Single
Caucasian
Investment Wholesaler
Protestant, then Presby-
terian for past year

Pam, 35, Single
Caucasian
Operations Manager for
Real Estate Company
Lutheran, then Unity
(Non-Denomination) for
past two years

Toney, 46, Married
Caucasian
Administrator for
Leadership Ministries
Mother, Wife
Born-again Christian for
the last sixteen years

From Chicago, Illinois:

Alicia, 31, Divorced
African American
Registered Nurse,
Mother
Baptist for twenty-
nine years, then
Christian (Non-De-
nomination) for past
two years

Anita, 26, Single
African American
Secretary
Baptist all her life

Annette, 52,
Married
Caucasian
Insurance Counselor
Roman Catholic all
her life

Beth, 28, Divorced
Caucasian
Clinical Social
Worker
Judaism all her life

Charlene, 48,
Divorced
Native American
Indian
Teacher
Traditional Native
American Indian and
Catholic

Cindy, 50, Divorced
Caucasian
Advertising
Protestant Christian, then
Judaism for past ten
years

Cynthia, 45, Widow,
Divorced
African American
Registered Nurse
Roman Catholic, then
Apostolic for past twenty
years

Diane, 38, Divorced
Caucasian
Hospital Administrator
Roman Catholic all her
life

Divna, 34, Divorced
Caucasian
Concierge
Eastern Orthodox all her
life

Hope, 43, Married
Caucasian,
Native American Indian
Nursing Administration
Protestant all her life

Jackie, 48, Married
African American
Manager
Baptist, then Roman
Catholic for ten
years, and now
Baptist

Jean, 30, Single
Caucasian
Design Training for
Software Company
Atheist, then Roman
Catholic for the past
year

Joan, 52, Divorced
Caucasian
Secretary
Roman Catholic all
her life

Julianne, 39,
Divorced
Caucasian
Director of Finance,
Work-Shop Coordi-
nator, Mother
Roman Catholic, then
no particular religion
for past twenty-two
years

Kate, 39, Divorced
Caucasian
Executive Secretary
to Vice President of
U.S. Firm

Roman Catholic all her
life

Leah, 30, Divorced
Caucasian
Pediatrician
Judaism and Roman
Catholic all her life

Mari Lee, 44, Single
Caucasian
Astrologer
Roman Catholic all her
life

Marilyn, 46, Divorced
Caucasian
Registered Nurse
Lutheran all her life

Marion, 74, Widow
Caucasian
Semi-retired
Roman Catholic now,
but Non-Practicing for
fourteen to twenty years

Mary, 91, Widow
Caucasian
Retired
Addressographer
Roman Catholic (Con-
verted at age twenty-
two)

Nancy, 45, Married
Caucasian
Service Provider in
a Hospital, Teacher,
Mother
Presbyterian all her
life

Nancy, 48, Single
Caucasian
Real Estate Sales-
person
No religious
affiliation

Peggy, 65, Single
Native American
Indian
Advisement
Coordinator for
Institute for Native
American Indian
Development
Traditional Native
American Indian
and Episcopalian

Regina, 39,
Married
African-American,
Native American
Indian
Registered Nurse,
Mother, Wife
Non-Denomination

Rita, 47, Single
Caucasian
Director of Parish
Councils, Registered
Nurse
Roman Catholic all her
life

Rose, 43, Divorced
African American
Mother, Secretary,
Word Processor
Baptist all her life

Rosetta, 50, Divorced
African American
Nurses Aide
Baptist

Ruth, 50, Divorced
Caucasian
Senior Vice-President
of Residential Sales,
Mother
Presbyterian and
Lutheran

Sally, 27, Single
Caucasian
Temporary Service
(Computer Specialist/
Word Processor)
Methodist, then Roman
Catholic

Susan, 45, Widow
Caucasian
Teacher
Judaism all her life

Susan, 46, Married
Caucasian
Nurse Researcher,
Coordinator of Quality
Assurance
Judaism all her life

Terry, 36, Single
Caucasian
Registered Nurse
Roman Catholic all
her life

Violet, 67, Widow
Caucasian
Retired Registered
Nurse
Lutheran all her life

Zander, 34, Single
African American
Secretary, Mother
Sanctified (Baptist)
for the past three and
a half years

Zenaida, 55, Widow
Asian, Philippine
Registered Nurse
Roman Catholic all
her life

*From the Northern,
Southern and Western
Suburbs of Chicago:*

Alice, 36, Single
Caucasian
Registered Nurse
Roman Catholic all her
life

Angela, 40, Married
Caucasian
Student, Observer
Roman Catholic, then
Lutheran for past
seventeen years

Bobbie, 57, Married
Caucasian
Service Representative
Roman Catholic all her
life

Bonnie, 29, Single
Caucasian
Account Service
Representative
Presbyterian all her life

Christine, 37, Married
Caucasian
Business Owner
Wife, Mother
Roman Catholic all her
life

Denise, 28, Single
Caucasian
Nurse Recruiter
Lutheran all her
life

Ellen, 47, Single
Caucasian
Technical Skills
Librarian
Protestant, now
Agnostic

Erna, 87, Widow
Caucasian
Retired Housewife
Lutheran all her
life

Evelyn, 52,
Married
African American
Wife, Registered
Nurse, Mother
Professional
Student
Baptist, then
Roman Catholic
for twelve years,
and now returning
to Baptist denomi-
nation

Ginny, 52, Widow
Caucasian
Customer Service
Representative

Roman Catholic, then
Methodist for past
fifteen years

Irma, 69, Widow
Caucasian
Homemaker
Roman Catholic, then
Born-again Christian for
past nine years

Jane, 28, Single
Caucasian
Nursing Management
Roman Catholic all her
life

Jennifer, 30,
Married
Caucasian
Sales
Wife, Mother
Roman Catholic all her
life

Karen, 46, Married
Caucasian
School Social Worker
Various Protestant
Religions, then Unitarian
Universalist for past
eight years

Kathleen, 41, Divorced
Caucasian
Dental Hygienist, Single
Parent
Presbyterian all her life

Lana, 44, Married
Caucasian
Supervisor, Wife, Mother
Roman Catholic, then Juda-
ism for the past twelve
years

Lorraine, 29, Single
Caucasian
Registered Nurse
Roman Catholic all her life

Marge, 60, Widow
Caucasian
Bookkeeper, Mother,
Grandmother
Roman Catholic all her life

Mary, 38, Married
Caucasian
Customer Service Man-
ager, Mother, Wife
Roman Catholic and
Lutheran for past four
years

Mary, 46, Married
Caucasian
Educator (Teacher Facilita-
tor), Wife, Mother
Unitarian Universalist for
past fourteen years

Mary Jane, 29, Married
Caucasian
Supervisor
Mother, Wife
Roman Catholic all her
life

Sandra, 38, Married
Caucasian
Customer Service
Supervisor of
National Accounts
Mother, Wife
Christian Science
then Roman Catholic,
and now Non-
Denomination
for past ten years

Sarah, 40, Married
Caucasian
Police Officer
Roman Catholic all
her life

Stephanie, 66,
Married
Caucasian
Housewife, Mother,
Grandmother
Roman Catholic all
her life

Sue, 44, Married
Caucasian
Registered Nurse,
Mother, Wife (order
depends on situation)
Lutheran most of her
life (Dropped out for
ten years)

Virginia, 55, Married
Caucasian
Security Officer, Mother,
Grandmother
Roman Catholic all her
life

From Quincy, Illinois:

Karen, 43, Married
Caucasian, Native
American Indian
Spanish Teacher,
Representative for Skin
Care Company
Mother
Pentecostal for the past
eleven years

Peggy, 40, Married
Caucasian
Teacher, Mother
Lutheran all her life

Victoria, 41, Married
Caucasian
Teacher, Mother
Roman Catholic all her
life

From Indiana:

Marsha, 40, Married
Caucasian
Hostess
Wife, Mother
Roman Catholic all her life

Mary, 62, Married
Caucasian
Secretary, Cashier
Homemaker, Mother
Protestant,
then Christian over
forty years

Mary Beth, 25
Married
Caucasian
Registered Nurse
Dutch Reform all her
life

Nancy, 38, Single
Caucasian
Registered Nurse
Protestant, then
Non-Denomination
for past eighteen years

Ruth, 56, Divorced
Caucasian
Office Manager for
Psychologists
Presbyterian, then
Christian Lutheran for
the past ten years

From Massachusetts:

Gerry, 54, Divorced
Caucasian
Teacher
Catholic all her life

From Missouri:

Francille, between
birth and death, Single
Caucasian
Educational Public
Relations
Protestant Methodist
all her life

From Oregon:

Valorie, 60, Divorced
Caucasian
Retired Waitress
No particular
denomination

From Wisconsin:

Patricia, 39, Single
Caucasian
Registered Nurse
Roman Catholic all her
life

From Washington, D.C.:

Jenae, 23, Single
Caucasian
Social Worker, Baker
Fundamental Christian
for eighteen years,
angry for two years,
then eclectic for past
four years

Home Is Where I Am:

Martha, 28, Single
Caucasian
Waitress, Artist
Roman Catholic, then
no religion affiliation
for past sixteen years

Appendix D
Interview Questions

1. Is spirituality important to you?

2. Does spirituality play a significant part in you life? Does it make a difference?

3. What does spirituality mean to you?

4. Do you consider yourself to be a spiritual person?

5. What forms your spirituality?

6. How did you learn about spirituality?

7. Was there a significant person in your life who taught you about spirituality? A significant female? A significant male?

8. How did spirituality develop in your life?

9. Do you practice through an organized religion? If so, does your organized religion help you connect with your spirituality?

10. Do your work experiences have an impact on your spirituality?

11. Are you aware of definite shifts in consciousness that have allowed you to expand your spirituality? If so, can you describe the significant incidents that caused your shifts?

12. Is it important to express your spirituality?

13. How do you express your spirituality?

14. When do you feel the most spiritual?

15. Has spirituality been difficult for you? If so, what was that difficulty?

16. How has spirituality eased your life?

17. Did you experience a barrier to your spirituality? If so, what was the barrier? What advice would you forward on to other women to overcome that barrier?

18. Has your spirituality had an impact with others in your life?

19. Do you discuss spirituality with your friends? Your family?

20. Do you feel spirituality is important for a female-male relationship?

21. Are men comfortable discussing the topic of spirituality with you? Are you comfortable discussing the topic of spirituality with men?

22. Is there a connection between your emotions and your spirituality?

23. Have you known women who seem to embody spirituality? If so, can you describe their spiritual characteristics?

24. If you had to give advice to men about spirituality, what would you personally tell them?

25. If you had to give advice to other women about spirituality, what would you personally tell them?

SHARE THE CONNECTION

Check bookstores everywhere or order here.

Toll-Free: 1-866-372-2636
secured online ordering
www.cameopublications.com

	# Items	Amount
Soul Awakenings: *Exploring The Spiritual Journeys of One Hundred Women* By Michelle A. Quigley Paperback (ISBN 0-9744149-2-1): **$19.95**		
Shipping: USA: $4.95 for first item; add $2.00 for each additional book SC residents please include 5% sales tax.		

Order Total

Please Print

Name: _____

Company: _____

Address: _____

City: _____ State: _____ Zip: _____

Phone: (____) _____

Cameo Publications, LLC
PO Box 8006
Hilton Head Island, SC 29938

Sorry no CODs

credit card # _____ expires _____

please sign _____